PRACTICAL PROGRAM EVALUATION FOR STATE AND LOCAL GOVERNMENTS

Second Edition

W0037980

by Harry P. Hatry,
Richard E. Winnie
and Donald M. Fisk

with contributions from:
Louis H. Blair,
Marvin R. Burt,
Alfred I. Schwartz
and Alease Vaughn

An Urban Institute Book

THE URBAN INSTITUTE PRESS · WASHINGTON, D.C.

This study was partially supported by funds from the U.S.
Department of Housing and Urban Development

Manufactured in the United States of America

LC 81-51346
ISBN 87766-296-7

9 8 7 6 5

Distributed by arrangement with

UPA, Inc.
4720 Boston Way
Lanham, MD 20706

This publication was printed by Braun-Brumfield, Inc.
from type set by Automated Graphic Systems

THE URBAN INSTITUTE is a nonprofit policy research and educational organization established in Washington, D.C. in 1968. Its staff investigates interrelated social and economic problems of urban communities, and government policies affecting those communities and the people who live in them. The Institute disseminates significant findings of such research through the active publications program of its Press. The Institute has two goals for work in each of its research areas: to help shape thinking about societal problems and efforts to solve them, and to improve government decisions and performance by providing better information and analytic tools.

Through work that ranges from broad conceptual studies to administrative and technical assistance, Institute researchers contribute to the stock of knowledge available to public officials and to private individuals and groups concerned with formulating and implementing more efficient and effective government policy.

Conclusions or opinions expressed are those of the authors and do not necessarily reflect the views of other staff members, officers or trustees of the Institute, or of any organizations which provide financial support to the Institute.

CONTENTS

PREFACE TO THE SECOND EDITION

Considerable activity in program evaluation has occurred since the publication of the first edition of this work in 1973. Numerous books and articles have been published, and at least two professional societies and a number of journals devoted principally to program evaluation have come (and sometimes gone). There have not, in our opinion, been any substantial developments in evaluation techniques, but there has been a growing recognition that the classic evaluation designs have limited applicability and pose more difficulties than commonly thought. Considerably more concern is being expressed over the usefulness of program evaluation and, thus, there is more attention to ways to make it more useful.

In addition, evaluations are beginning to be conducted for state and local governments, some by consultants, some by the governments themselves. Some state and local governments now have separate evaluation units, while others have assigned evaluation activities to existing analytic organizations, legislative audit units, or budget agencies.

All of these developments since the first edition make it clear that a second edition is warranted. This edition differs from the first mainly in the following respects:

- The addition of a new chapter on how evaluation can be used to improve the future performance of the program being evaluated, which is—or at least should be—one of the major objectives of state and local program evaluation.
- The inclusion of suggestions for relating outcome data to workload characteristics and program operating characteristics in order to improve the usefulness of evaluations by providing an improved perspective on program impacts.
- Greater emphasis on assessing a program's evaluability prior to initiating a full evaluation.
- Expanded discussion of regular outcome monitoring of programs as an adjunct to special in-depth program evaluation. Regular outcome monitoring is becoming a major activity in many state and local governments. We believe outcome

monitoring should be considered a major program evaluation strategy.

- Somewhat more emphasis on assessing programs' efficiency (productivity) in addition to the traditional focus on program effectiveness.
- The addition of an appendix that discusses the conditions under which controlled, randomized experiments are most likely to be applicable to state and local governments.

In addition, we have added a number of new examples. Some of these are substitutes for the original ones, but we have retained many of the original examples because of their effectiveness in illustrating desired points. We also have made many revisions in phrasing where we felt the original wording could be improved.

As with the first edition, this one does not attempt to say all that is known about program evaluation. The volume is highly selective; the goal is to provide an understanding of essentials. We hope this will encourage readers to explore the many other excellent materials currently available that offer in-depth discussion of program evaluation. Nonetheless, this volume continues to be somewhat unique in its orientation to state and local issues and the amount of space it devotes to the selection of evaluation criteria, ways to collect data for an evaluation, and the institutional issues involved in implementing program evaluation.

One of the virtues of the first edition was its conciseness. This second edition has been expanded, but we hope that readers will continue to find the book direct, succinct, and practical.

Harry P. Hatry
Richard E. Winnie
Donald M. Fisk

ACKNOWLEDGMENTS

The authors wish to acknowledge the considerable assistance provided by the following people who made suggestions and reviewed drafts of the first edition of this report (the affiliations listed were those at the time of their assistance): George A. Bell, Council of State Governments; Professor Donald T. Campbell, Northwestern University; Mark L. Chadwin and James Kent, Illinois Economic and Fiscal Commission; Jerry B. Coffman, City of Charlotte, North Carolina; Richard Lehne, U.S. Department of Housing and Urban Development; Keith E. Marvin, General Accounting Office; David Seidman, District of Columbia Government; John Surmeier, Georgetown University; Carol H. Weiss, Bureau of Applied Social Research, Columbia University; C. Edward Wise, U.S. Department of Housing and Urban Development; and Louis Blair, Garth Buchanan, Michael Flax, Joseph Lewis, Nelson McClung, Cornelius P. McKelvey, Robert Sadacca, Philip Schaenman, Alfred Schwartz, Joseph Wholey, and Richard Zamoff of The Urban Institute.

A number of additional people provided information on state or local evaluations that have been used as examples in this second edition. They include Pat Manion and Paul Swenson of the city government of Phoenix, Arizona; Tom Finnie and Pam Syfert of the city government of Charlotte, North Carolina; Laurie Stryker, Jim Clark, and Larry Polivka of the state government of Florida; Henry Brillinger of the state government of Pennsylvania; Reginald Carter of the state government of Michigan; and Ray Pethtel of the Commonwealth of Virginia's Joint Legislative Audit and Review Commission. Alfred Schainblatt of The Urban Institute provided a number of helpful suggestions to improve the new edition.

SUMMARY

Evaluating the effectiveness of programs in meeting public objectives is an essential component of state and local government management. This report is intended to help state, county, and city governments improve their program evaluation capabilities. It is aimed at the government analyst—both at the central staff and operating department level—as well as the overall manager or administrator.

Most evaluations today focus primarily on inputs and the management process rather than on how the program affects its clients and the public at large. Attempts to identify systematically both the positive and negative effects of specific programs on the general public or on specific population segments are seldom made.

Systematic program evaluations, by themselves, will not necessarily point the way to payoffs in better or less expensive programs. Nevertheless, proper evaluations appear to have considerable potential for providing much better guidance than presently exists for decisions on whether specific programs should be modified, expanded, or dropped. Evaluation can be especially important in helping to test programs in their early stages before large commitments of resources are made. In addition, evaluations in some instances can suggest ways for improving program performance.

The first steps in evaluation are to identify specific program objectives (including the reduction of unintended and unwanted effects), specify criteria for measuring progress toward these objectives and the magnitude of program effects, and identify the population segments that are likely to be affected by the program and on which program impact data should be assembled. This report contains suggestions for accomplishing those tasks.

Various evaluation designs are then discussed. Each is a framework for analyzing data concerning a program's impact in order to estimate the changes that can be attributed to the program. These evaluation designs vary in their cost, their degree of complexity, and the precision with which they isolate program effects. The use of simpler and less expensive approaches is emphasized to keep evaluation feasible for state and particularly local governments. An often omitted but vital step in evaluation is to look explicitly for factors, other than the program, which may have caused the results shown by the data. Wherever feasible, the use of comparison or control groups similar to the group served by the program is highly recommended. This allows clearer identification of the effects related to the program rather than to external factors.

The procedures for collecting evaluation data are a vital concern. A number of procedures—in addition to using statistics from existing records—are discussed. For example, interviews of citizens can produce valuable insight into aspects of a program's effects and unintended consequences that are not otherwise obtainable. Interviewing former clients of treatment programs with hoped-for long-term impacts (such as health, drug abuse, alcoholism, corrections, and employment training programs) can provide vital information on the effectiveness of these programs. Lack of such follow-up is a major weakness in current evaluation efforts.

Furthermore, innovation and advance planning can reduce data collection costs and improve the usefulness of the evaluation. For example, to reduce the cost of data collection, conclusions can often be based on a sample of events or a sample of clients. It is important, however, that such samples be carefully drawn to represent accurately the entire population of interest.

It is usually preferable to plan an evaluation prior to the program's implementation. This often allows data collection procedures to be incorporated in normal program operations, thereby reducing the need for special data collection. In addition, advance planning may create opportunities to collect data that would not be obtainable retrospectively. For example, advance planning allows collection of client perceptions of their condition at the start of service, which can subsequently be compared to their perceptions after services have been provided.

A formal program evaluation process is recommended for states and for local governments of more than 100,000 population. Government officials should conduct program evaluations according to an annual plan or scheme so as to provide a basis for allocating staff for the evaluations. Otherwise, evaluation will likely be a haphazard process, with evaluation personnel frequently being diverted to help resolve day-to-day emergencies. The selection of topics for evaluation should include consideration of whether a meaningful evaluation is likely to be feasible, whether the program has actually been in place long enough for a successful evaluation, and the probable usefulness of evaluation results in future program operating and budgetary decisions. The work schedule of the evaluation should insure that findings are available in time for important program decisions. Explicit provision should be made in the schedule for briefings of appropriate program and central-staff personnel about the findings. If the evaluation clearly shows a need for governmental action, the evaluation report should be followed by the development of a specific plan of action.

The evaluation process should include two types of evaluation (perhaps with about half of the resources available for evaluation applied to each):

1. Outcome monitoring. An annual review of selected outcomes should be conducted for each major service or program (solid waste collection, health, etc.). Such regular monitoring of key indicators can indicate generally whether program-related conditions are improving, worsening, or remaining constant. The emphasis is on highlighting changes and trends without necessarily attributing them to past government activities.

2. Ad hoc evaluation. Selective, individual, in-depth evaluations of programs should be conducted to measure changes produced by the programs. The emphasis is on identifying impacts due to the particular program being evaluated. Criteria for selecting which programs to evaluate are presented in this report.

To assure reasonable objectivity and establish credibility, it is preferable that control of the evaluation rest with an office other than the one directly responsible for operating the program. Central-staff review of evaluation plans and monitoring of major evaluation activities is desirable when the evaluation is undertaken by an operating agency.

Special effort should be undertaken to make evaluations useful to the operating agencies responsible for the evaluated programs. Ways to do this include examining the relationship of outcomes to the program's major characteristics and to the character of the program's workload. This might be done either as part of the original evaluation design or later in the evaluation, when particular characteristics surface as potentially having an important relation to outcomes. Even if only crude technical procedures are used, such information can identify program characteristics that are associated with less satisfactory outcomes and thus provide clues to program officials about possible program changes.

Obtaining an experienced professional who can direct the work and provide training to others involved in the evaluation is an important priority. Government salary structures are a major constraint here, although the universities are producing an increasing number of graduates interested in government and educated in the technical skills needed for evaluation. Where specialized skills are required, outside consultants can be used to fill gaps, to provide on-the-job training to internal evaluation staff, or to undertake complete evaluations.

The program evaluations discussed in this book require from approximately three staff-months of effort for the simpler evaluations to two or more staff-years for the more complex studies. It is sometimes estimated that one-half to 5 percent of program funds should be provided for evaluation purposes. Such estimates are rough guidelines at best. State and local governments should include an evaluation component in their proposals for federal funding whenever possible; federal agencies often are supportive of such efforts. In the final analysis, the evaluation effort should offset its cost by demonstrating how to keep program costs down or by showing how to increase program effectiveness.

There are a number of technical and other limitations to program evaluations, including the willingness and ability of political officials to modify or eliminate ineffective programs that have developed a large or vocal clientele. Nevertheless, selective use of program evaluation has the potential for considerably strengthening state and local government decision making.

PRACTICAL PROGRAM EVALUATION FOR STATE AND LOCAL GOVERNMENTS

I. SCOPE AND CURRENT PRACTICES

Evaluating the effectiveness of programs is a basic part of good management. Managers of all types of organizations, both public and private, need feedback to guide future decisions regarding continuation of modification of their organization's activities.

Unfortunately, too many state and local governments do not obtain the feedback necessary to measure program effectiveness. Thus, they have little basis for judging whether a specific program is working as planned or how well it is serving the public. Information, where it does exist, usually is sketchy and inadequate for decision making.

Furthermore, state and local governments (especially the latter) encounter serious obstacles when they attempt to assess their program, including:

- limited resources, both in staff time and dollars;
- tight deadlines for completing the assessments—often within a few months, if not weeks; and
- pressure to divert available evaluation staff to tangential purposes like "firefighting."

Obstacles like these often result in poorly planned, superficial evaluations. The challenge to state and local governments is to develop an evaluation capability that can be responsive to many of the more immediate needs of decisionmakers and yet be able to provide relevant and technically adequate evaluations.

This report is intended to provide a guide to state and local governments interested in developing their program evaluation capabilities and to provide basic suggestions for conducting practical and systematic program evaluations under conditions of highly limited evaluation resources. It tries to be useful to the spectrum of state, city, and county agencies, including central administrative offices, operating agencies, state and local legislative review units, and performance audit agencies.

Although the illustrations are drawn from jurisdictions with large populations (the states, cities over 50,000 population, and counties over 100,000 population), the concepts presented should also be useful to smaller governments.

The impetus for program evaluation has come from the academic community and the federal government. A considerable body of excellent literature on evaluation and its techniques has sprung up.[1] But the lessons learned from the work undertaken so far have, for the most part, not been discussed from the perspective of state or local government. This book attempts to help fill that void.[2]

What Is Program Evaluation?

Program refers to an activity or group of activities undertaken by a government to serve the public. A program is usually conducted by a single agency, but sometimes it requires the meshing of efforts by various government and private agencies. Program evaluation is the systematic examination of a specific government program to provide information on the full range of the program's short- and long-term effects. While a program evaluation may include consideration of workload measures, operating procedures, or staffing, its chief focus is on measuring the program's impact.

Evaluation aimed solely at a program's internal procedures, staffing, and management, without assessing impacts, is better labeled process evaluation.[3] Also excluded from our definition of program evaluation is the process of developing alternatives to existing programs to estimate the likely future effects of these alternatives.

Program evaluation, as defined here, focuses on the past performance of ongoing or completed programs; thus, it is primarily retro-

---

1. See, for example, References 8, 10, 13, 18, 35, 38, 43, 48, 49, 51, and 54. Each provides a good grounding in program evaluation techniques.

2. Attempts to address program evaluation from a state or local perspective can be found in References 11, 28, and 34.

3. Information from process evaluations can be very useful for identifying possible reasons for low performance and thereby suggesting needed program changes. In addition, before the program evaluation begins there should be at least a brief examination to make sure that the program is actually in place. See the discussion in Chapter 6 on the selection and scheduling of programs to be evaluated. We suspect that state and local governments will prefer evaluations that are a combination of process and impact evaluation, with the process evaluation used to identify major problems and to make suggestions for their correction. For further discussion of this linkage, see Chapter 5.

spective. Program evaluation, however, also provides data for estimating the future effects or costs of the programs evaluated.

Program evaluation concentrates on outcomes, identifying how public conditions or individual citizens and population groupings have changed as the result of a specific program or set of activities. Some of the possible subjects of program evaluation are shown in Exhibit 1.

A program evaluation attempts to measure the degree to which a program is achieving its intended public purposes and is having positive and negative impacts. Consequently, the evaluation helps policy officials decide whether a program should be continued, expanded, modified, reduced, or eliminated. If a program is not performing as desired, the evaluation may help indicate the reasons for ineffectiveness and the actions that might be taken to remedy the situation.

For example: A study by the city of Nashville, Tennessee, on the care of neglected and dependent children prior to court disposition contained an evaluation of the existing child care system. This study showed that a large number of children were assigned to the government child care institution for several weeks before they were subsequently returned to their homes by the court. It became apparent that proper screening of children at intake and the provision of 24-hour emergency child care service in the home would eliminate the need to remove many children from their homes to an institution, thereby avoiding the trauma that accompanies such relocation.[4]

A Special Type of Program Evaluation: Outcome Monitoring[5]

Regular monitoring of the status of major programs can be considered to be another kind of program evaluation, called outcome monitoring.

The effectiveness of major programs (such as criminal apprehension, treatment of mental illness, fire protection, transportation, recreation, and waste collection and disposal) probably should be monitored at least annually, even if only in crude fashion. Each service should be examined to identify its positive and negative

---

4. See Reference 56.

5. This type of evaluation is sometimes called performance measurement.

Exhibit 1. POTENTIAL APPLICATIONS OF PROGRAM EVALUATION

The following might be the subjects of individual program evaluations:

Crime Control

- An altered mix of forces such as a major change in the proportion of foot patrols, one-officer police cars, two-officer police cars, plainclothes patrol officers, detectives, etc.
- A neighborhood team policing program
- Reallocation of police by geographical location, time of day, or day of week
- New communication devices

Fire Control

- New fire control procedures, equipment, or vehicles
- New communication devices
- Reallocation of firefighters and equipment by time of day or geographical location

Highway/Street Lighting

- New types of lighting in certain parts of the community

Solid Waste Collection

- New collection equipment
- New types of refuse containers

Solid Waste Disposal and Water Treatment

- New equipment or procedures

Recreation

- New recreational programs, e.g., opening school grounds on weekends
- Selected existing programs and activities

Employment Programs

- New types of training programs
- A new job generation and matching program

Exhibit 1 (continued)

Transportation

- Revised traffic control arrangements
- Revised public transit routings or new bus lanes
- New road maintenance materials or equipment

Health

- Various drug abuse treatment programs
- Changes in the hours or location of maternal and infant care clinic
- Special publicity campaigns for attracting persons to VD clinics, or alteration of clinic location or hours of operation

Housing Code Enforcement

- Various enforcement practices

Note: Education is often relatively independent of state, city, and county governments and therefore has not been included in this list. However, there are many potential applications of program evaluation to educational activities.

---

impacts on citizens. Key indicators should be used to measure the effectiveness of these services. These data, reviewed annually, can provide government managers with information on the status of each major service and highlight deficiencies and problem areas. When compared over time, such information indicates trends and areas needing corrective action.

This monitoring differs somewhat from the usual concept of program evaluation. While in-depth, ad hoc, program evaluations attempt to identify the effects that can be attributed to specific programs, outcome monitoring concentrates on showing program-related outcomes and how they have changed over time. Outcome monitoring, in other words, is not an attempt to determine what role a government program has played in reaching a specific outcome; it does not separate the impact of a particular program from changes which may have resulted from other events (for example, changes in local economic conditions).

Outcome monitoring may also be an appropriate way for a government to start developing a program evaluation capability by providing the type of data base needed for successful evaluation. Also, because it is less detailed and does not require large expenditures, it can provide management with the type of data needed for effective government-wide monitoring. Monitoring can be used for a larger number of government programs than program evaluation, but it provides less information about the extent to which government activities have been the cause of the outcomes.

Outcome monitoring, however, can help to identify government activities that warrant in-depth program evaluation—that is, programs whose outcomes appear to be unsatisfactory or are worsening. Much of the discussion in the remaining chapters applies to outcome monitoring as well as to in-depth, ad hoc, program evaluations.

Present Methods of Assessing Performance

Most elected officials and government managers periodically undertake some form of program review. These reviews are usually of the following types:

- Discussions with Program Managers. This is probably the most common type of review. These discussions usually fail to provide agency heads or the central administrator with crucial information needed for decisions about the program. Complete objectivity cannot be expected from managers defending their own operations and budgets. Furthermore, the discussions usually center on the manner in which programs are undertaken and dwell on immediate workload data, such as tons of waste collected, number of cases handled, or miles of streets or highways repaired or maintained. Thus, the effects of the program on the public are often neglected.
- Examination of Program Statistics. Program statistics usually cover such items as the number of parks or recreational facilities maintained, the number of vehicles and sanitation workers in the program, and the tons of garbage collected by area. The problem here, as above, is that most of the data focus on inputs rather than outputs. In addition, these statistics do not reflect the effect of the program upon the public, such as citizen satisfaction with park and recreational facilities or how much clients improved after receiving social services. In some cases, available statistics—such as crime rates, the number of fires and the amount of the financial loss from them, the number of traffic accidents and the resulting injuries and fatalities—provide some idea of outcomes. Even in these cases, however, the changes in data from one time period to another are seldom systematically related to specific programs.

- Applying Professional Standards. In some programs, such as health and recreation, professional standards are sometimes available for assessment purposes. These standards are usually expressed in terms of the quantity or types of inputs required for satisfactory service. Examples of such standards are the number of hospital beds per capita, the acres of recreational area per capita, and the case load targets for parole, probation, and social service case workers. While this information can be useful in program evaluation, it falls short of indicating the effects of programs on citizens.
- Reviewing Citizen Complaints. A common type of evaluation, especially in local governments, is to examine complaints by citizens (although a surprising number of governments still do not tally complaints by subject matter). These complaints are not likely to be representative of the total community. Many people do not complain because they don't want to cause trouble, don't want to spend the time to do so, or feel it would be useless. Legitimate complaints also may not reach government attention because some citizens do not know how to file a complaint. It is difficult to judge the extent of a problem on the basis of complaints alone. The problem may be the concern of a vocal few or be shared by many more who have not spoken up.

These types of review fail to provide important information about a program's effects on the community and its citizens. They tend to have the following drawbacks:

- They focus on inputs or on the process of managing the program. They seldom focus on the full range of outputs—that is, on the level and quality of service received by citizens and the community.
- The procedures used to gather information are often unsystematic and catch-as-catch-can. Thus, the information available may not represent actual conditions.
- The shortage of time and staff prevents meaningful, thorough assessment.
- Even when outputs are reviewed, the review tends to cover only a small part of the consequences of a program.

Current methods of program review also overlook two important characteristics of government services.

First, public services seldom affect all segments of a community's population in the same way. The current types of program review rarely distinguish between impacts on particular segments of the population and the population as a whole. The community as a whole may be well served by a program, but certain neighborhoods may be receiving inadequate service. A recreation program, for example, may inadvertently ignore the special needs of aged, very young, or handicapped persons. Furthermore, a program with generally positive effects may actually be detrimental to some parts of the community. Thus, careful evaluation of the impacts on various subgroups should be an important part of program evaluation.

Second, some programs—such as health, employment, or corrections—seek to provide long-term benefits. Once a person has left these programs, however, governments seldom attempt to find out whether the results were successful in the long term. Without such follow-up, evaluation of these programs must rely on short-run information, such as the number of patients discharged or the proportion of trainees that had a job at the time a job-training program ended.

The newer government budgeting systems—including program budgeting; planning, programming, and budgeting-type systems (PPBS); and, more recently, zero-based budgeting—have stimulated greater interest in systematic evaluation. Federal government efforts have provided additional encouragement. Some federal legislation provides that a portion of the appropriations for selected government programs be used for formal evaluation. Most federal agencies have established program evaluation units.

Interest by Congress and U.S. General Accounting Office (GAO) led GAO to develop a set of audit standards in 1972.[6] Focusing on program results as well as costs and efficiency, these standards are intended to be useful to state and local governments. This broad concept of auditing goes well beyond that normally undertaken—and into the area of program evaluation.

A number of state governments have introduced some form of performance or program audits or legislative evaluation.[7] In addition, "sunset" legislation in many states now mandates periodic review of the achievements of at least some state agencies.

---

6. See Reference 46.

7. References 66, 68, 69, 79, and 80 are examples of the growing number of audit-type program evaluations.

Why the Lack of Comprehensive Evaluations?

Despite these recent improvements, the magnitude of evaluation efforts remains small. There are understandable reasons for the lack of comprehensive program evaluation in state and local governments:

- Evaluations can be expensive and time consuming. Funds and staff are often not readily available, and the idea that evaluations may result in lower total costs or increased program effectiveness has not been widely accepted. This is partly because the payoffs of evaluation have not been widely demonstrated or advertised.
- Many managers believe that "the value of my program cannot be measured." In one sense, they are right: The results of programs cannot be measured precisely. However, at least partial and practical means are available for measuring the impact of most major programs, and new methods for gathering necessary data are being developed.
- Explicit, systematic program evaluation can be controversial. Program managers and citizen groups who support the programs being evaluated may be defensive and protest negative evaluations.
- State and local governments often have lacked personnel who are skilled in quantitative techniques and analysis. This problem is being remedied as improved training materials become available and as graduate schools of business and public administration place greater emphasis on quantitative methods. Increasingly, graduates entering government today are equipped with sufficient background to undertake most of the work involved in program evaluation. However, certain aspects of program evaluation may require specialized skills such as statistics.
- The quality, timeliness, and impact of evaluations (including federally sponsored evaluations) generally have been poor.[8]

The Scope of this Report

This report is designed to help governments that intend to conduct program evaluations, whether internally or by outside consul-

---

8. References 21, 26, and 52 are examples of published materials containing critiques of past evaluations.

tants. Regardless of who conducts the evaluation, the government manager needs to know when and how to request an evaluation, how to make sure that the evaluation is comprehensive and reliable, and how to place the evaluation information received in perspective.

This report does not examine in detail the specific techniques or the conceptual basis for program evaluation. Rather, it briefly covers the points most likely to be of concern to government personnel. It focuses on approaches that will be relatively inexpensive but that will provide information adequate for most state and local government purposes. It is probably not necessary that evaluations conducted for local or state governments conform to the standards of professional experimenters and evaluators. As long as systematic procedures are followed (from identifying objectives to data analysis) and the findings are properly stated, the information received from program evaluation can provide officials with valuable help.

Not every program evaluation will be useful. A certain percentage of them will probably have to be aborted because conditions changed in the middle of the evaluation; others, though completed, will provide results that are too ambiguous to be of much use. Despite hazards like these, most systematic evaluations, thoughtfully done, should provide an improved basis for making decisions concerning the programs evaluated and amply compensate for the time and resources required.

Chapters 2, 3, and 4 present the basic steps in conducting program evaluation. Chapter 2 discusses program objectives, associated evaluation criteria, and clientele groups for whom the criteria should be measured. Chapter 3 outlines various "evaluation designs" that show how the comparisons that make up the evaluation can be structured. Chapter 4 describes the major techniques for obtaining data and the problems associated with data collection.

Chapter 5 provides suggestions on steps that can be added to an evaluation so that it can be used to improve the program evaluated. Chapter 6 discusses the institutional issues of organization, staffing, costs, presentation of results, and follow-up.

Appendix A is a case study that illustrates some of the evaluation tactics presented in previous chapters and illustrates how they are tied together. Appendix B discusses the conditions under which controlled, randomized experiments are most likely to be appropriate for state and local governments.

II. WHAT'S THE PROGRAM ALL ABOUT? IDENTIFYING PROGRAM OBJECTIVES, EVALUATION CRITERIA, AND CLIENTELE GROUPS

Three elements of program evaluation are discussed in this chapter: (1) identification of program objectives, (2) identification of appropriate evaluation criteria (or "measures of effectiveness") for which data should be sought, and (3) identification of relevant population segments or clientele groups. These elements are interrelated. In practice they can and probably should be considered jointly. These basic steps apply both to outcome monitoring and to in-depth, ad hoc, program evaluation.

Officials requesting a program evaluation should make sure that all relevant objectives, criteria, and clientele groups are included in the evaluation so that the evaluation will be sufficiently comprehensive.

The following sections provide some guidelines for selecting objectives, criteria, and client groups.

Identify Objectives and Evaluation Criteria that Are People Oriented

The objectives and criteria should reflect the potential impacts of a program on citizens and the community (or state). Unfortunately, there is an understandable tendency to concentrate on those effects that are easiest to measure such as the workload accomplished— tons of garbage collected, number of cases handled, or number of persons processed at intake—and on the short-term effects of a program, such as how many clients in a health program show improvement at the time of discharge or how many clients in a training program complete the program.

These data may be useful for explaining certain aspects of a program's success or lack of it, but in themselves they say little about the extent to which citizens and the community are helped by the program. The objectives and the evaluation criteria should cover the public conditions that the programs are designed to affect (for example, the objectives and the evaluation criteria should encompass the

13

potential effects of the program on citizen health, public safety, and the quality and perceived satisfaction of citizens with the service).[1]

Consider Explicitly the Unintended Consequences of Programs, Particularly Possible Negative Effects

For most programs, an explicit objective should be to reduce the program's negative consequences. This objective, however, is generally neglected. Instead, objectives are usually expressed as intended, beneficial effects.

Some examples of potential unintended results of programs that need to be examined are the following:

- The noise, air pollution, and community disruption that may result from major road-building programs.
- A reduction in the amount of low-income housing available in a community as a result of urban renewal or housing code enforcement programs.
- Increased street litter and street crime caused by new recreational programs for youth.

Most programs are likely to have some negative effects, and many, if not most, programs are likely to have effects (both beneficial and detrimental) that are not anticipated. Specific evaluation critiera should cover such negative effects, even if some are not detected until after the evaluation has begun.[2]

The purpose of explicitly including negative effects is not to retard progress but to place the program's overall worth in proper perspective and to encourage the designing of programs that reduce such negative consequences.

---

1. References 17, 20, 23, 24, 25, 32, 39, and 53 are examples of attempts to identify people-oriented measurements for a number of state and local government services.

2. The identification of unintended effects is the focus of "Goal-free Evaluation." Goal-free evaluators, however, go beyond unintended effects to conduct "an evaluation of outcomes without the evaluator being exposed to, or contaminated by, knowledge of the purposes or goals." See Reference 41. Though we strongly encourage the explicit search for unintended effects and the consideration of these in evaluations, it seems excessive for evaluators to avoid exposure to formal goal statements. Sole reliance on goal-free evaluation may miss consideration of important objectives that have not been accomplished. For an excellent discussion of goal-free evaluation, see Reference 22.

Include Evaluation Criteria Even Though There Are Apparent Difficulties in Measuring Them

Evaluation criteria should be identified without any initial concern as to whether, or how, they can be measured. As will be discussed in Chapter 4, there are often ways to measure, at least partially, the more qualitative, subjective evaluation criteria (for example, through the use of ratings, rankings, or other procedures).

Consider Multiple Objectives and Evaluation Criteria

Rarely are a single program objective and a single evaluation criterion sufficient to describe the impacts of a program. Virtually every program has numerous objectives, and numerous evaluation criteria will be needed to measure a program's effects.

Exhibits 2 and 3 are examples of statements of objectives and related evaluation criteria. They were originally prepared for use by governments in annual outcome monitoring. However, criteria for outcome monitoring generally will be applicable to program evaluations, and vice versa.

Exhibits 4 and 5 illustrate evaluation criteria that were used in individual program evaluations—one of drug abuse treatment programs and the other of a crime control program.

It is probably better initially to err on the side of including too many objectives, evaluation criteria, or clientele groups than to eliminate some that might be important when examined more closely. Neither public officials nor program evaluators should eliminate a potential evaluation criterion (or clientele group) on the basis of their own personal observation.

Separate the Program's Effects on Different Population Groups

Different groups within the population may be affected to different degrees by a program. It is important to identify such groups and to collect data reflecting the program's impacts on them. An average crime rate or an average family income will not reflect the possibly major differences that may exist among segments of the population. The following points should be considered:

- Each program will have a group or groups that are the intended beneficiaries, that is, clients of the program.

Exhibit 2. RECREATION OBJECTIVES AND ASSOCIATED
EVALUATION CRITERIA

OBJECTIVES

To provide all citizens, to the extent practicable, with a variety of leisure opportunities that are accessible, safe, physically attractive, and enjoyable.

EVALUATION CRITERIA

1. Overall Citizen Rating: (Overall Satisfaction)
   a. Percentage of households that feel recreation opportunities are very good
   b. Percentage of households that feel recreation opportunities are poor

2. Overall User Rating: (Enjoyableness)
   a. Percentage of user households that feel recreation opportunities are very good
   b. Percentage of user households that feel recreation opportunities are poor

3. Crowdedness: (Enjoyableness)
   a. Percentage of user households that feel that amount of facility space is poor

4. Facility Upkeep: (Physical Attractiveness)
   a. Percentage of "poor" ratings by trained observers making weekly ratings of facility appearance.
   b. Percentage of user households that feel facility cleanliness is poor
   c. Percentage of user households that feel maintenance of equipment is poor

5. Helpfulness—Attitude of Staff: (Enjoyableness)
   a. Percentage of user households that feel attitude of staff is poor

6. Hours of Operation: (Accessibility)
   a. Percentage of user households that feel hours of operation are poor

7. Safety: (Safety)
   a. Percentage of user households that feel safety is poor
   b. Number of serious accidents per 100,000 hours of use
   c. Number of deaths per 1,000,000 hours of use

Exhibit 2 (continued)

8. Participation: (Enjoyableness)
   a. Percentage of citizens who have used a government facility or program one or more times during a given time period
   b. Percentage of citizens who have not used a government facility or program one or more times during a given time period, categorized by reason for nonuse

9. Attendance: (Enjoyableness)
   a. Total annual attendance at government facilities or programs

10. Hours of Attendance: (Enjoyableness)
    a. Total citizen attendance hours at government facilities or program

11. Physical Accessibility: (Accessibility)
    a. Percentage of citizens who live within x miles of a government recreation facility

12. Variety: (Variety)
    a. Average number of different programs per facility

Note: The word or phrase in parenthesis is the objective to which the specific evaluation criterion most directly applies.

Source: Adapted from Reference 17. Reference 17 and 24 describe detailed data collection procedures for these criteria.

- Each program is likely to significantly affect certain other groups, even though they are not the intended beneficiaries. These effects may be detrimental or beneficial.
- Some types of clients may be more difficult to help than others.
- The citizens of the community, or of a state considered as a whole, often comprise a category that should be explicitly identified; especially for services that affect all citizens, such as public safety and street cleaning programs.
- In some cases, future citizens may be an important group to consider explicitly.

A list of characteristics for classifying clientele groups that are usually important in state and local government programs is presented in Exhibit 6. In addition, each program is likely to have some unique clientele groupings. Some examples of clientele groups for individual programs are presented in Exhibit 7.

Exhibit 3. TRANSPORTATION OBJECTIVES AND ASSOCIATED EVALUATION CRITERIA

OBJECTIVES

To provide access to community services, facilities, and employment in a safe, quick, comfortable, and convenient manner for all segments of the community without causing major harmful side effects.

EVALUATION CRITERIA

Accessibility and Convenience

1. Percentage of residents not within x distance of public transit service and more than one hour from key destinations
2. Percentage of citizens rating convenience of public transportation as "poor"

Travel Time

3. Average time required to travel between key origin and destination points
4. Congestion—duration and severity of delay

Comfort

5. Road surface quality ("rideability") index
6. Citizen perception of travel comfort

Safety

7. Rate of transportation-related deaths, injuries, and incidents of property damage
8. Number of public transportation crime incidents

Minimum Cost to Users

9. Cost per trip

Maintenance of Environmental Quality

10. Noise levels along transportation corridors and number of persons at risk
11. Air pollution attributable to transportation sources and number of persons at risk

General Public Satisfaction

12. Citizen perception of adequacy of transportation services

Monetary Costs

13. Program Costs

Source: Adapted from Reference 53. References 53 and 24 also suggest data collection procedures for these criteria.

Exhibit 4.   EVALUATION CRITERIA: EVALUATION OF
DRUG ABUSE TREATMENT PROGRAMS[a]

Long-term Rehabilitation of Former Clients

1. Number and percentage who were addicts or abusers on entering treatment and who became drug abstinent or relatively free of drugs for various lengths of time
2. Percentage who were unemployed on entering who are now employed or in school and increase in client-months/year devoted to gainful employment or formal education
3. Change in annual arrest rates on felony and drug charges from the year before entering treatment to the year after leaving treatment
4. Improvement in physical and mental health
5. Percentage who re-enter treatment

Short-term Rehabilitation of Current Clients

6. Client retention rates
7. Percentage of clients using illicit drugs during treatment
8. Number and percentage of clients graduating from treatment
9. Percentage of clients arrested on drug or felony charges during treatment
10. Percentage of clients becoming employed or re-entering school during treatment
11. Percentage of clients with unauthorized breaks in treatment

Overall Drug Abuse Control System

12. Percentages of persons arrested in the jurisdiction who are drug addicts or who are under the influence of drugs
13. Number of drug overdose deaths
14. Total number of addicts

a. The program evaluation from which this exhibit is drawn was part of a study not only to assess the existing performance of drug treatment programs but also to examine options for improving the drug treatment system.

Source: Reference 57.

Include Dollar Cost as One Criterion

Although cost analysis is not always discussed in publications on program evaluation, it is clear that state and local governments will want to know how much the program has cost. Program costs can then be compared with program impacts. The cost figures can also

---

Exhibit 5. EVALUATION CRITERIA: EVALUATION OF
POLICE TAKE-HOME CAR PLAN

1. Number and rate of crimes of various types—especially those potentially deterrable by the presence of a police car in the vicinity

2. Crime clearance (arrest) rates

3. Number of traffic accidents, injuries, and fatalities[a]

4. Index of citizen feeling of security

5. Index of police-community relations

6. Index of police morale

7. Program costs

Note: An evaluation of the Take-Home Car Plan in Indianapolis is documented
      in Reference 62. In the plan, police officers were assigned a marked police
      car for their full-time use while both on and off duty so that some marked
      police cars were on the streets at all times. The program evaluation was
      concerned with the changes in these criteria attributable to the operation
      of the program. The evaluation focused on criteria 1, 2, 3, and 7 because it
      was too late to obtain data for criteria 4, 5, and 6 on preprogram conditions.

a. Although reduction of traffic accidents was not the initial focus of the program,
   accidents may be significantly affected by the program; hence, they were included in the criteria.

Source: Reference 62.

---

be used to derive estimates of likely future costs if the program is
continued. Estimating program costs is more complex than is generally recognized and is discussed briefly in Chapter 4.

Service efficiency (productivity) has become a major concern of
state and local governments. Efficiency criteria are likely to become
considerably more important in the future. There is no reason why
program evaluations cannot assess program efficiency as well as
program effectiveness.

The typical measures of efficiency are unit-cost ratios, such as
"cost per unit of output." (The term "productivity" is usually
applied to the reciprocal, e.g., "number of units of output per dol-

---

Exhibit 6.   TYPICAL POPULATION/CLIENTELE GROUP
CLASSIFICATION CHARACTERISTICS

1. Residence location—grouped by neighborhood, service area, pre-
   cinct, etc., for local governments; or by county, region, planning
   district, etc., for states[a]

2. Sex

3. Age—groups such as young people and the elderly may have particular needs relevant to certain programs

4. Family income group—often the poor have special needs

5. Racial/ethnic group

6. Special-handicap group

7. Education level

8. Home ownership and type of dwelling

9. Employment status

10. Family size

a. Residence location can sometimes be used as a proxy for some of the other
   socioeconomic characteristics.

---

lar.") For program evaluations, the unit of output should be meaningful and be of a specific level of quality. The measure "cost per
client helped" is preferable to "cost per client served;" "cost per
complaint resolved satisfactorily" is preferable to "cost per complaint handled."[3]

Possible Ways of Identifying Program Objectives, Evaluation Criteria, and Clientele Groups

Although it is rare to find program objectives, evaluation criteria,
and clientele groups neatly described and packaged, important clues

---

3. For further discussion of efficiency measurement issues, see Reference 23 and
   Chapter 16 of Reference 24.

Exhibit 7.   EXAMPLES OF CLIENTELE GROUPS FOR
             PARTICULAR SERVICES

Type of Service	*Clientele Groups*
Solid Waste Collection	Persons living in various locations Low-income families Elderly and physically handicapped persons Residents of single vs. multiple housing units Residential vs. commercial users
Recreation	Persons living in various locations Sex Age Persons with special handicaps Persons without access to an automobile Low-income families Users of particular types of activities, e.g., golf, tennis, and hiking
Drug Abuse Treatment	Addicts of various lengths of time and types of habit; age, sex, income class, and race Potential addicts Families of addicts; of potential addicts Citizens as a whole, particularly as potential victims of drug-related crime
Transportation	Persons living in various locations Persons without access to an automobile (including the very young, the elderly, housewives without an automobile, persons who cannot afford one or who do not want to drive) Persons with physical handicaps Low-income families

about them can be found through a number of sources, particularly the following:

- Legislative statements about program objectives and evaluation criteria. These are usually available on programs originated at the federal or state level; these statements are rarely all-inclusive, however, and often are vague.

- Statements made by legislators or citizens at hearings or in the press.
- Discussions with program personnel, who will often be aware of many unintended as well as intended consequences, both beneficial and negative, as well as the various population segments that appear to have been affected.
- Discussions with government officials themselves. (It may be argued that too explicit a statement of objectives may at times be politically dangerous. Officials may have hidden agendas which, for one reason or another, they believe are not appropriate to identify. Nevertheless, in most program evaluations, evaluation criteria and objectives can and should be explicitly identified. If there is too much hidden agenda, the formal program evaluation is likely to lack utility and should not be attempted in the first place.)
- Interviews with a small number of clients of a specific program. These can be an important way of identifying criteria against which to assess a program.
- On-site observations of the delivery of the service by the evalutors themselves.

Exhibit 8 contains a set of questions that might be asked by evaluators to help identify program objectives, evaluation criteria, and program clients.

Exhibit 8.   QUESTIONS TO HELP IDENTIFY OBJECTIVES, EVALUATION CRITERIA, AND CLIENTELE GROUPS

1. What is intended to be changed by the program, both immediately and in the long run? How would the program manager know if the program is working? What evidence would be accepted as indicating "success"?

2. What are the possible side effects, both immediate and long run?

3. Who is the target of the program? What types of people? Is the community as a whole affected, either directly or indirectly? Who else might be affected by the program?

4. What would be the consequences if the program were eliminated? What would happen to the citizens in the community? Who would complain? Why would they complain? Who would be glad? Why?

A Summary Exercise

A useful exercise is to identify appropriate evaluation criteria for some of the items listed in Exhibit 1. Let us take street lighting as an example.

Suppose that a government has installed special street lighting in one section of the community primarily to reduce crime. It is now in the process of deciding whether to expand the program, and if so, whether modifications are desirable. Clearly, the program evaluation should include estimates of the *amount of crime* that has been deterred by the improved lighting. In addition, citizen *feelings of security*, particularly citizens living in the vicinity of the special lighting, would be another useful criterion. However, street lighting also has other potential effects. It may reduce *traffic accidents;* thus, the number of accidents and injuries would be relevant criteria. Another possible, though unintended, effect of street lighting may be a reduction of *neighborhood attractiveness.* Unsightly or excessive lighting may harm the appearance of the neighborhood or bother the residents, for example, by making it harder to sleep in homes facing the lights. These possibilities should also be considered. *Program cost,* as always, is a relevant criterion.

III. COMPARISON—THE NAME OF THE GAME

This chapter discusses the next major step in conducting a program evaluation—how to estimate what changes can be attributed to the program being evaluated rather than to nonprogram factors.

This chapter does not, in general, apply to annual outcome monitoring of specific services or programs, since attributing change to specific programs is too ambitious an undertaking for outcome monitoring. (Data from outcome monitoring can be useful, however, for individual program evaluations.)

Ideally, we would like to compare what actually happened with what "would have happened if the world had been exactly the same as it was, except that the program had not been implemented." But since it is impossible to determine exactly what "would have happened if . . . ," the answer to the problem is to use procedures that will give us an approximate idea of what would have happened.

This chapter presents five evaluation designs for identifying and quantifying program effects. They are the following:

1. *Comparison of "before" and "after" data*
   Compares program results measured at two points in time: the period before the program was implemented, and at some appropriate time after implementation.
2. *Comparison of time trend projection of preprogram data with actual postprogram data*
   Compares actual postprogram data with estimates projected from a number of time periods prior to the program.
3. *Comparison with population segments not served by the program*
   Compares data from segments of the population toward whom the program is directed with data on other segments of the population not served by the program.
4. *Controlled, randomized experimentation*
   Compares similar preselected groups, some of whom are served by a program and some of whom are not (or are served in different ways). The critical factor is that the comparison groups

25

are systematically assigned (before program implementation) so that, except for the program, they are as similar as possible.

5. *Comparisons of planned vs. actual performance*
Compares actual, postprogram data with targets set prior to the time period covered by the evauation.

Exhibit 9 illustrates the comparisons basic to the first four of these designs. Although the fifth is not usually considered an evaluation design, it is discussed in this chapter because of its potential interest to state and local officials.

The major function of program evaluation is to identify the changes in the values measured by the evaluation criteria that can reasonably be attributed to the program. A major problem is that other governmental programs or external events occurring during the time period covered by the evaluation, and not the program being evaluated, may have been the reason for the observed changes.

All but the first and the fifth designs include explicit provisions for "controlling" for at least some of these other factors. Nevertheless, in all cases there should be an explicit and thorough search for other plausible explanations of change. Abnormal weather conditions, other public or private programs with the same, or similar, objectives, special characteristics of the served population not originally recognized, and other factors may affect program results.

In the following section, each evaluation design is summarized as to the procedures involved, applications, costs, and special problems associated with each.

Design Number 1: The Bargain Basement Approach—Comparisons of "Before" and "After" Data

This first design is the simplest type of evaluation except possibly for Number 5. It identifies changes brought about by the program as differences between the values of the evaluation criteria measured before, and an appropriate period after, the program's introduction (See Exhibit 9, Design 1.) Of the first four designs, it is probably the most common, but it is the least capable of distinguishing between the impacts of a particular program and impacts stemming from other causes.

The steps in this evaluation design are as follows:
• Identify relevant objectives and corresponding evaluation criteria.

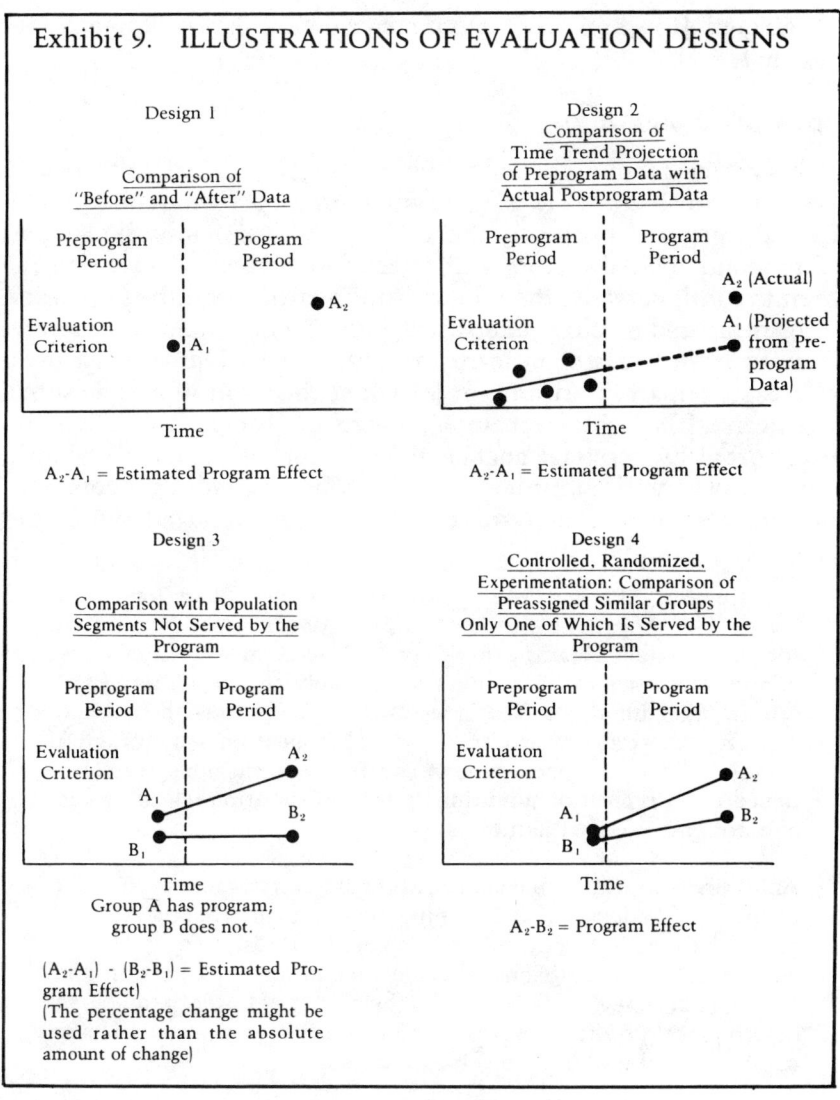

Exhibit 9. ILLUSTRATIONS OF EVALUATION DESIGNS

Design 1

Comparison of
"Before" and "After" Data

A₂-A₁ = Estimated Program Effect

Design 2
Comparison of
Time Trend Projection
of Preprogram Data with
Actual Postprogram Data

A_2-A_1 = Estimated Program Effect

Design 3

Comparison with Population
Segments Not Served by the
Program

Group A has program;
group B does not.

$(A_2-A_1) - (B_2-B_1)$ = Estimated Program Effect)
(The percentage change might be
used rather than the absolute
amount of change)

Design 4
Controlled, Randomized,
Experimentation: Comparison of
Preassigned Similar Groups
Only One of Which Is Served by the
Program

A_2-B_2 = Program Effect

- Obtain the values for these criteria for the period before the program's introduction and for the period since introduction.
- Compare the before and after data to estimate the changes brought about by the program.
- Look for other plausible explanations for the changes. If there are any, estimate their effect on the data or at least identify them when presenting the findings. (This last step is often ne-

glected. It is, however, a vital step to making this design credible.)

Types of Application

This design often is the only type that is practical when time and personnel are limited. It is most appropriate (1) when the period covered by the evalution is short (thus making it less likely that nonprogram related factors will affect the evaluation criteria); (2) when the link between the program intervention and the outcomes being measured is close and direct so no other major events are likely to have had a significant influence on the values measured with the evaluation criteria; or (3) when the conditions measured have been fairly stable over time (and are not, for example, likely to be distorted by seasonal changes[1]), and there is reason to believe such stability will continue. Otherwise, before and after comparisons may reflect short-term fluctuations rather than program-related changes.

Washington, D.C., used this design to evaluate its Operation Clean Sweep. (See Appendix A for a description of this evaluation.) This intensive street-cleaning program extended over a nine-week period. No other major changes were likely to affect the output criteria. Neighborhood cleanliness was measured just before and just after the program through a visual inspection system and a survey of citizens' perceptions. The before conditions were believed to be typical of conditions prior to Operation Clean Sweep and not of a seasonal nature.

An example at the state level is a State of Pennsylvania evaluation of vocational education and training programs in state prisons. Pre-prison jobs and earnings were compared to postprison jobs and earnings. The comparison indicated that in-prison education and training had a negligible impact on the ability of former inmates to obtain jobs. In addition, postprison jobs seldom were found to have made use of the training received in prison.[2]

---

1. If the before and after periods do not include the same months of the year, the evaluators will have to take possible seasonal effects into account. Even without a new program, for example, conditions are likely to be better during certain seasons.

2. See Reference 70.

This evaluation design contains an implicit assumption that the values for the evaluation criteria just before the program was instituted are the best estimates of what the values would have been without the new program.

This design (like the others) will generally be more effective if the evaluation is planned prior to program implementation. Such pre-planning will permit the collection of special data to provide adequate evaluation criteria. For example, the evaluation of Operation Clean Sweep used special inspections of street cleanliness before the program began. The data normally collected by a government will seldom be adequate for this type of evaluation.

Many times, much can be learned from a careful, systematic examination of a program and at least its immediate, short-term consequences, even if a more elaborate evaluation design is not used. The following are examples of this:

> To evaluate changes made in procedures for the scheduling of clients in its food stamp program, San Diego County, California, collected before and after data on (a) client waiting times, (b) percentage of clients required to return to a welfare center with additional documentation, (c) number of days between client's application and day the client was authorized to purchase food stamps, (d) error rates, and (e) number of clients processed per day. Substantial improvements were found on all five criteria. Attribution of the changes to the program seemed reasonable for several reasons: the program changes introduced were quite plausibly directly linked to the evaluation criteria, the timing of the program changes was closely linked to the time of the changes in the values of the evaluation criteria, and no other major explanations were apparent.[3]

> Examination of Nashville's system for precourt disposition of neglected and dependent children showed that 60 percent of the children temporarily placed in the county's facility were returned to their own homes as soon as the court acted. This suggested excessive reliance on institutional care prior to the court's review and led to correction action to provide noninstitutional short-term emergency care.[4]

> Phoenix, Arizona, tested a new refuse collection system in one neighborhood of 440 households. A formal evaluation was part of the test. The new system used a mechanical loading system at-

---

3. See References 78 and 83.

4. See Reference 56.

tached to refuse collection trucks to transfer refuse to the trucks from 30- or 90-gallon containers provided by the city and shared by households. The system was found to require considerably fewer trucks and personnel and reduced overall collection costs. Visual inspection was made of the amount of alley litter in the test neighborhood and in an adjacent neighborhood where refuse continued to be collected as it had been before. A questionnaire was sent to each household in the test area by mail four months after the test began. Returns were received from 80 percent of the households who evaluated such aspects of the new collection method as its appearance, convenience, and odor. The responses were generally positive. As a result of the evaluation, the city moved ahead to full-scale implementation.[5]

Cost

This is the least expensive of the five designs except for Number 5. If the evaluation is based solely on data customarily collected by the jurisdiction, its cost is likely to be quite low. Special data collection will increase the costs, the amount of the increase depending on the collection procedures used. In addition to the special inspections of streets, the evaluation of Operation Clean Sweep involved a small telephone survey both before and after the program. These added several thousand dollars to the cost of the evaluation, but without this added expenditure the evaluation would have been much less useful.

Design Number 2: Comparison of Time Trend Projection of Preprogram Data with Actual Postprogram Data[6]

This design compares actual postprogram data on the evaluation criteria with projections for the criteria based on data from previous years. The changes caused by the program are identified as the differences between present-day conditions and what they would have

---

5. See Reference 73.

6. In some situations, projections based on factors other than, or in addition to, time trends may be appropriate. For example, the population may have changed significantly during the period covered by the evaluation. Rather than using the preprogram values of the evaluation criteria (such as crime rates), projections of crime rates might be made based on the current population mix. These projections would then be compared with the crime rates after a crime prevention program was introduced.

been if the program had not been instituted—as estimated by the projections. (See Exhibit 9, Design 2.)

The steps in this evaluation design are as follows:

- Identify relevant objectives and corresponding evaluation criteria.
- Obtain data on each of the criteria at several intervals prior to the program and after implementation.
- Using statistical methods and the data from preprogram years, make projections of the values of each of the criteria to the end of the time period covered by the evaluation.
- Compare the projected estimates with postprogram data to determine the amount of change resulting from the program.
- Look for plausible explanations for changes in the data other than the program itself. If there are any, estimate their effect on the data or at least identify them when presenting the findings.

Types of Application

This design is useful where adequate historical data are available and where there appears to be an underlying trend (upward or downward) over a period of time that would seem likely to have continued if the new program had not been introduced. The statistical projections may not be meaningful, however, if the data for prior years are too unstable. If there is strong judgmental evidence that underlying conditions have changed in very recent years, data on prior years should probably not be utilized.

Crime or accident statistics, for example, may rise or fall for individual years, but when many years are considered together a trend may be apparent. Comparison of data from one preprogram year with postprogram data may be influenced by extremes and thereby be misleading. The projection of a trend to the time of the evaluation and comparison with postprogram results will indicate whether the trend has been altered by the new program.

> This design was used to evaluate the Indianapolis, Indiana, Take-Home Car Plan. Under the plan, marked police cars were provided to police officers for their full-time use. For the evaluation, traffic accident rates and crime rates (especially for those crimes most likely to be deterred by police cars) were obtained for each of six years prior to the plan. A statistical projection was made and compared with the crime and traffic accident rates that occurred after the plan's implementation. Exhibit 10 shows some of the time series and projections. Exhibit 11 shows the summary table com-

32

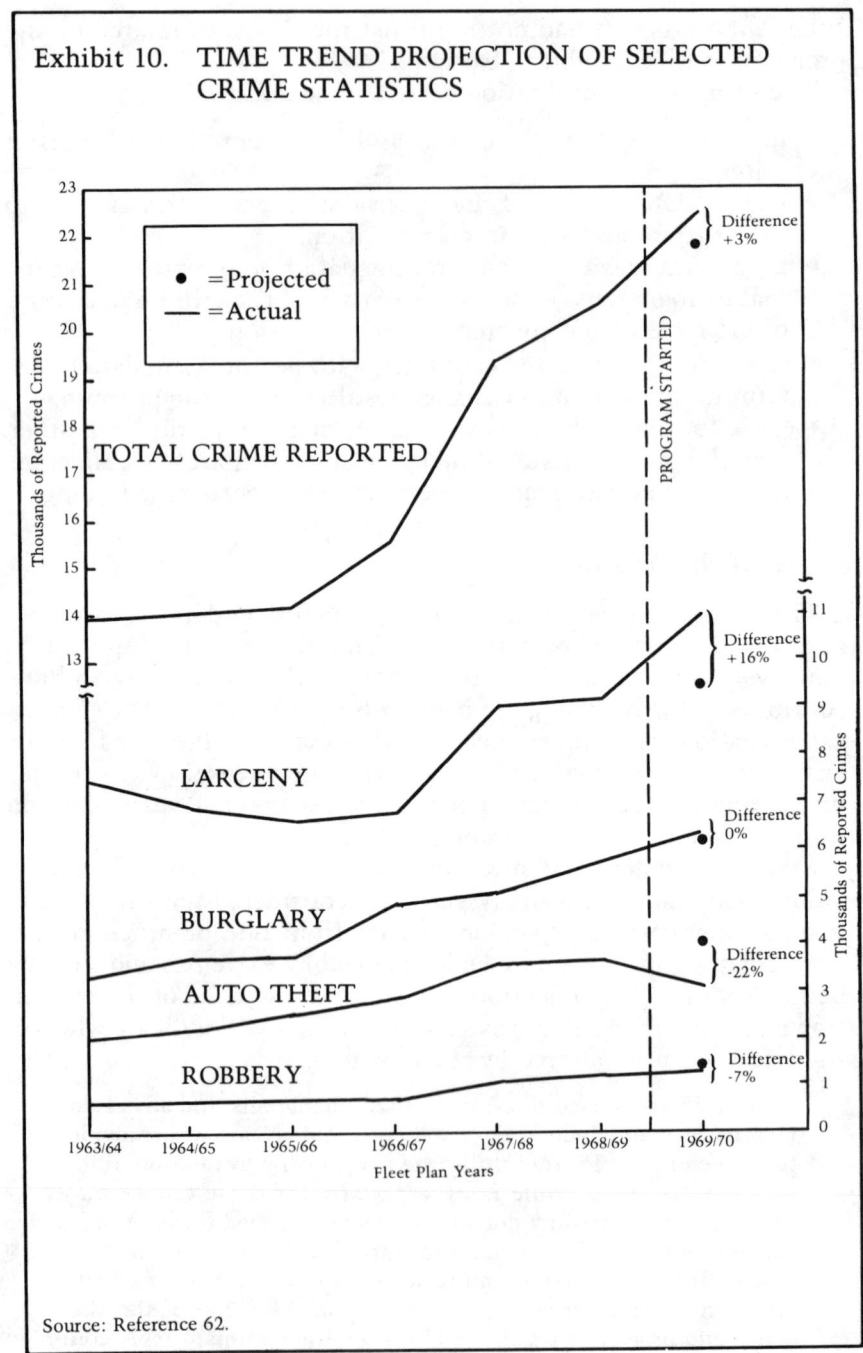

Exhibit 10. TIME TREND PROJECTION OF SELECTED
CRIME STATISTICS

Source: Reference 62.

Exhibit 11. SUMMARY OF INDIANAPOLIS POLICE TAKE-HOME CAR PLAN—EFFECTS AND COSTS

A. Reported Crime, Clearance Rates and Traffic Accident Records, 1969/70,[a] Compared with Projections Based on Previous Trends

	Projected Result Without Plan[b]	Actual Result With Plan	Percent Difference
Reported Crime (in numbers)			
Total Crime	21,798	22,451	+ 3
Larceny	9,458	10,996	+16[c]
Burglary	6,281	6,308	0
Robbery	1,294	1,207	− 7
Outdoor Crime Index	7,467	6,431	−14[c]
Purse Snatching	306	241	−21[c]
Street Robbery	820	762	− 7
Theft from Auto	2,420	2,378	− 2
Auto Theft	3,921	3,050	−22[c]
Clearance Rates (in percent)			
Total Crime	21	22	+ 5
Larceny	17	20	+18
Burglary	20	17	−15
Robbery	27	27	0
Auto Theft	23	26	+13
Vehicle Accidents (in numbers)			
Total Accidents	10,846	9,356	−14[c]
Killed	60	40	−33[c]
Injured	4,197	4,000	− 5

B. Cost of Plan Operation[d]

Initial Investment	$650,000
Subsequent Annual Cost	
Equipment Replacement	$200,000
Operating Expense	250,000
Total	$450,000

a. Based on the "plan year" comprising September, October, and November of 1969, and January, February, March, April, and May of 1970.
b. Projection based on trends from 1963 through 1969, using months of "plan year."
c. Indicates that change is significant according to standard statistical test.
d. Full-year cost.

Source: Reference 62.

paring projections with actual results. (The findings of any such evaluation could be summarized in this form.)

Exhibit 10 also illustrates the problem of unstable series data. Both the total crime reported and the larceny extrapolation time series are volatile. Consequently, projections based on these figures should be used with considerable caution.[7]

Data on more than one time period since program implementation would have provided considerably more evidence as to whether a significant change in trends had occurred.

Cost

This design has two additional elements that increase the costs relative to Design Number 1: a need for technical expertise to undertake the statistical projections, and the collection of data on prior years. The latter requires special attention to see that the data are comparable with current data.

Design Number 3: Comparisons with Population Segments Not Served by the Program

This design compares the values of the evaluation criteria of either (a) a jurisdiction having the program with a similar jurisdiction or jurisdictions not having the program, or (b) within a jurisdiction, a population segment served by a program with a population segment or segments not served by the program. (See Exhibit 9, Design 3.) If the other population segments show similar changes over time, it is probable that factors other than the new program were responsible for the change.

The steps in this evaluation design are:

- Identify relevant objectives and corresponding evaluation criteria.
- Identify other, similar, population segments not being served by the program.
- Obtain data on each of the criteria for each of the population segments being compared from before implementation of the program through the period covered by the evaluation.

---

7. For excellent discussions of the nature of the problems in this and similar types of designs, see References 9, 10, and 13. Note also that statistical projections could include consideration of nonlinear as well as linear forms.

- Compare the changes in the values of the criteria for those population segments served by the program with changes in values of the criteria for segments not served. Compare rates of change as well as amount of change.
- Look for plausible explanations for changes in the values other than the program. If there are any, estimate their effect on the data or at least identify them when presenting the findings.

Types of Application

This design offers some protection against attributing change to a specific program when external factors that affect many local, or state, governments or population segments within a jurisdiction are responsible for bringing about the change.

> With respect to the Indianapolis Take-Home Car Plan, for example, the introduction of a new ignition lock system nationally at about the same time might have significantly affected auto theft rates. Selected comparisons with other jurisdictions and with the nation as a whole, however, showed that the auto theft rate went down in Indianapolis while it continued to rise in other parts of the country. This strongly suggests that the national ignition lock program was not a significant factor in the Indianapolis reduction.

> The evaluators of the Connecticut program to enforce speed limits also used this design. The program was evaluated in part on its effectiveness in reducing the number of traffic fatalities per 100,000 population. Although initial inspection of the data indicated a decline in fatalities coinciding with the introduction of the program, the evaluators could not exclude the possibility that other nonlocal factors, such as improved vehicle safety, national safety advertising, or weather conditions might also have caused the decline. The evaluators then compared Connecticut's fatality rate with fatality rates in neighboring states. This comparison showed that Connecticut's fatality rate declined relative to neighboring states, thereby indicating that some factor unique to Connecticut was having an effect on fatality rates. Exhibit 12 shows this comparison.[8]

This design can be applied when a comparison group can be identified for which (a) data on evaluation criteria can be obtained, and (b) the group appears sufficiently similar to the program being evaluated that meaningful comparisons can be made. This design should

---

8. See Reference 9.

Exhibit 12.   CONNECTICUT AND CONTROL STATES:
TRAFFIC FATALITIES PER 100,000
POPULATION, 1951-1959

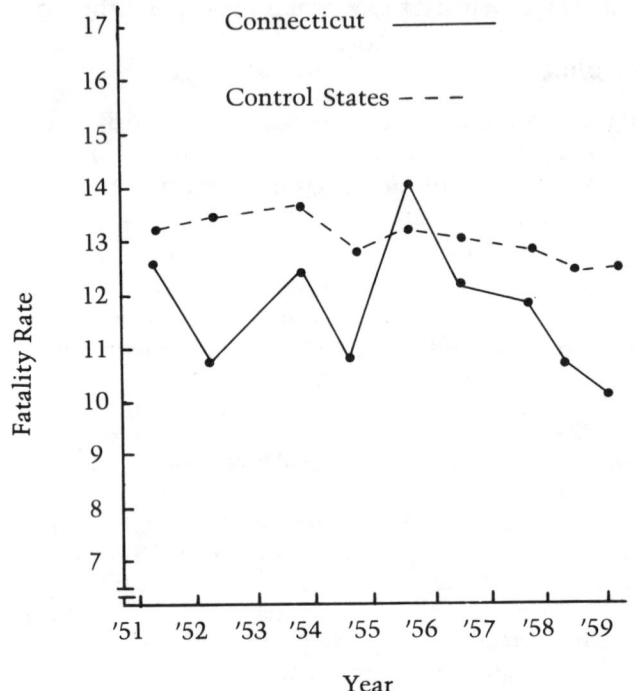

Note: Speed-limit enforcement program was introduced in Connecticut in Fiscal
       Year 1955-56

Source: Reference 9.

be considered when controlled, randomized experiments are not feasible (see Design 4 and Appendix B).

An important variant of this design occurs if a program is divided into a number of variations. The clients of these variations can be considered as comparison groups. A state supervising a number of county programs, for example, might find important service delivery variations among them that should be compared. If some counties do not implement any version of the program, the no-program counties also can be compared with the counties with program variations. Local governments might compare program variations in different police, fire, or solid waste collection districts, or variations in library or recreational facilities.

In an evaluation of alternative programs for treating alcoholism in Alameda County, California, a no-treatment comparison group was not available. Instead, the program that provided the least amount of treatment—detoxification only—was used as the comparison group. Statistical adjustments were made (using regression analysis) for certain client characteristics (age, sex, income before treatment, alcohol-related arrests before treatment, years of heavy drinking, daily consumption of alcohol, and whether client was receiving public assistance). The evaluation report, however, also noted that "no amount of technical sophistication can control for the one single factor that may go farthest to explain the outcomes: client motivation."[9]

An example of the use of statistical analysis as a major component of an evaluation is the following:

The State of Pennsylvania wanted to evaluate the effect of state police traffic patrols on traffic accidents but decided that it would be too expensive to systematically alter patrol levels in order to approximate a controlled experiment. Instead, the evaluators obtained data for eighteen patrol zones on accidents per mile (the dependent variable) and several independent variables, including patrol hours per mile per day, radar hours per mile, total arrests per mile, and traffic volume. Correlation analysis and multiple regression analysis were used to assess relationships among variables.

Volume of traffic was found to explain a large proportion of the variation in accidents (about 65 percent of the variation), but arrests and patrol hours were also found to have a significant relation. A 1 percent increase in traffic volume was associated with a 1 percent increase in traffic accidents; a 1 percent increase in patrol hours, and a 1 percent increase in traffic arrests were each associated with about an 0.2 percent decrease in traffic accidents.[10]

Special Problems

Identifying comparable jurisdictions or similar population segments within a jurisdiction is a particularly difficult problem. Con-

---

9. See Reference 55.

10. See Reference 72.

siderable caution needs to be exercised in identifying comparison groups and interpreting the findings.

> An evaluation of treatment programs for drug addicts in Dade County, Florida, for example, compared the effectiveness of a methadone program with a program of residential therapeutic communities for addicts. An essential element was the need to consider differences in client characteristics—such as age, sex, extent of addiction, arrest records, and motivation as indicated by the amount of screening done by each program—to see whether the clients were at least roughly similar.[11]

Without random assignment of clients to the various groups (as called for in Evaluation Design Number 4), the groups may be significantly different. Motivation and personality of clients, for example, can differ among the groups being compared, and such differences can be difficult to identify.

An evaluation of drug treatment programs, for example, may have the problem that persons who voluntarily enroll in treatment programs are likely to have different motivations and different personal characteristics than those who did not volunteer. Some programs may have skimmed off the cream of the persons needing treatment; other programs may have much less success in dealing with persons less highly motivated.

In situations where the comparison groups are to be clients of other agencies or other organization units, it is also preferable that past performance levels be roughly similar for the treatment and comparison agencies. Otherwise, the findings from the evaluation can be confounded by whatever factors led to the initial differences in performance levels.

A major danger of this design—not having comparision groups that are sufficiently comparable—is illustrated by the following examples:

> Wilmington, Delaware, evaluated alternative approaches to motor vehicle maintenance, focusing on police cars. Twenty-nine vehicles were assigned to each of four variations: three involved various forms of preventive maintenance, while the fourth omitted any preventive maintenance. The principal evaluation criteria were repair cost per mile and downtime per mile. Unfortunately, the types of cars assigned to each maintenance mode differed. When the results were analyzed, it was found that the fourth group (no preven-

---

11. See Reference 57.

tive maintenance) contained newer cars. The results of the evaluation changed when the same age cars were compared, but to do this, the number of cars in some groups became too small to provide reliable results.[12]

The State of Florida evaluated a program to divert problem children from the juvenile justice system. The evaluation compared diverted youths with youths who had been placed on probation by examining the recidivism rates of a random sample of about 350 in each group. The diversion group was found to have better outcomes. Major differences in age and prior arrest record between the two groups, however, raised a substantial question about the accuracy of the aggregate comparison. Fortunately, when the data were categorized by age and prior record, the originally observed, aggregate advantage of the diversion program remained.[13]

These examples illustrate the importance of examining available data on characteristics of the groups to identify any significant differences among the groups that would affect their comparability.

Although this design helps to control for some important external factors, it is generally not a fully reliable measure of program effects. It is best used along with other designs.

Use of this design for interjurisdictional comparisons depends on the availability of comparable data on the evaluation criteria from other jurisdictions. Limited availability of comparable data may be a difficulty. The type of data collected, and the care with which they are collected, are likely to vary among jurisdictions.

Cost

This design includes two elements not included in either of the first two evaluation designs. Effort is needed to identify similar jurisdictions or population segments and to collect comparable data about them. If the evaluation relies on already available, standardized data sources (e.g., uniform crime reports), the costs of data collection will be small. If special data collection efforts are required (to gather or verify data), the cost may be considerably higher.

---

12. See Reference 81.

13. See Reference 63.

Design Number 4: The Cadillac of Program Evaluations—Controlled, Randomized Experimentation

This evaluation design is by far the most powerful. Unfortunately, it is also by far the most difficult and most costly. It assesses the effectiveness of a program by systematically comparing specific changes in carefully identified groups of clients. One group is served by a program, while the others are not. (See Exhibit 9, Design 4.) This design can also be used to assess variations of a program to determine which is the most effective. This results in more groups to be compared.

The basic evaluation design consists of the following steps:[14]

- Identify relevant objectives and corresponding evaluation criteria.
- Select the groups to be compared, i.e., the control and the experimental groups. Members of the population of interest (or a probability sample of that population) are usually assigned in a scientifically random manner to one of the groups. This maximizes the likelihood that the groups will have similar characteristics.
- Measure the preprogram values for the evaluation criteria of each group.
- Apply the program to the experimental group but not to the control group.
- Monitor the program and the control group to see if anything happens that might distort the findings (such as the behavior of program personnel toward one of the groups). If appropriate and possible, such occurrences should be corrected. If that is not possible, the occurrences should at least be identified and their impact on the findings estimated.
- Measure the postprogram values for the evaluation criteria of each group.
- Compare the preprogram and postprogram values for the evaluation criteria of the groups to determine what differences in performance have occurred.
- Look for plausible explanations for differences in performance between the two groups due to factors other than the program.

---

14. We do not attempt to discuss the many technical steps in controlled, randomized experiments. A number of the listed references are excellent sources of such information, especially References 8, 10, 13, 18, 35, 38, 43, 48, 49, 51, and 54.

The randomization called for in the second step protects against this to a considerable extent. Nevertheless, there remains the possibility that other factors, perhaps occurring during the experiment, may affect one group and not the other in some special way.

Types of Applications

Traditionally, Design Number 4 has been suggested for use in evaluating programs designed for specific individuals, e.g., health or employment program. This design should also be considered for a variety of treatment programs, such as health, drug or alcohol abuse, corrections, and rehabilitation. Exhibit 13 is a checklist of the conditions under which controlled, randomized experiments are likely to be most appropriate. These conditions are discussed in more detail in Appendix B.

Phoenix, Arizona, used a controlled experiment to help evaluate its Alcohol Safety Action Program (ASAP). Problem drinkers referred to the program by the courts for driving while intoxicated were randomly assigned (by a court employee) to one of three types of treatment. The three types differed in terms of educational and therapeutic effort. Follow-up, in-person interviews were conducted with about 190 clients of the program in the sixth, twelfth, and eighteenth month after entry. Data on a number of criteria were obtained, including amount of drinking, employment status, physical health, and extent of drinking-related problems. The courts opposed the use of a no-treatment control group, so the minimum-treatment group was used as the control group. The interviews were conducted by several part-time ASAP employees who received approximately ten hours of training. Federal funds supported the evaluation effort.[15]

The District of Columbia Bail Agency conducted an experiment to determine the effects of the degree of supervision of persons charged with felonies who had been given conditional releases prior to trial. For two months in 1975, 300 defendants were randomly assigned to one of three levels of supervision (100 to each level). At the lowest level of supervision, the defendants themselves initiated contacts with supervisors. The second level of supervision involved biweekly telephone calls or letters to defendants. The highest level of supervision involved monthly visits by the supervisor to the defendant's residence or place of employment.

---

15. See Reference 74.

Exhibit 13.   CONDITIONS UNDER WHICH CONTROLLED, RANDOMIZED EXPERIMENTS ARE MOST LIKELY TO BE APPROPRIATE

1. There is likely to be a high degree of ambiguity as to whether outcomes were caused by the program if some other evaluation design is used.

2. Some citizens can be given different services than others without significant danger or harm.

3. Some citizens can be given services different from others without violating moral or ethical standards.

4. There is substantial doubt about the effectiveness of the program.

5. There are insufficient resources to provide the program to all clients.

6. The risk in funding the program without a controlled experiment is likely to be substantially greater than the cost of the experiment; the new program involves large costs and a large degree of uncertainty.

7. A decision to implement the program can be postponed until the experiment is completed.

8. Experimental conditions can be maintained reasonably well during the experimental period.

9. The findings are likely to be generally applicable to a substantial proportion of the population of interest.

10. Sufficient staff and dollars are available to manage the experiment.

11. Client consent for participation in the experiment is not required or, if it is, can be obtained without invalidating the experiment.

12. The confidentiality and privacy of the clients involved can be adequately maintained.

Data on the outcome of the experiment were collected two years later, after all the cases had been disposed of by the court. The outcomes assessed were pretrial crime as indicated by rearrest rates, failure-to-appear rates, and compliance with conditions of release (such as maintaining regular contact with the bail agency and refraining from contact with complaining witnesses). The rearrest rates showed no significant difference (overall, about 26 percent of the defendants were rearrested, but a slightly higher percentage of those under intensive supervision were rearrested, that is, 28 percent). The group under intensive supervision did somewhat better than the other two groups on the other two measures. The agency reported that the experiment was conducted with relatively little difficulty. It felt that the major reasons for the success of the experiment were the availability of sufficient resources to design, implement, and evaluate the experiment, and staff continuity over the two-year period.[16]

To assess its employment and training program, the Michigan Department of Social Services randomly assigned 231 clients not served by existing employment programs to one of two groups. Those in the experimental group were given employment, educational, and training opportunities. Those in the control group were left to pursue employment opportunities on their own. Each client was interviewed by phone between six and ten months later about their experiences in finding employment. The experimental group was found to be more successful in finding jobs as compared to the control group for those persons who had the fewest barriers to employment (e.g., who had transportation or who were not handicapped).[17]

An important variation of Design Number 4 for state and local government purposes is comparison of program effects in different geographical areas. Many programs can be varied geographically, for example, be initially introduced in some geographical areas of a community and not in others. For state evaluations, a program can be introduced in some counties and not in others. In local governments, for example, new crime control, traffic control, firefighting, or solid waste collection procedures might be (and sometimes are) initially tried out in a few areas of the jurisdiction. Areas with similar characteristics would be identified, and some of the areas would then be randomly selected as program participants.

---

16. See Reference 61.

17. See Reference 65.

For example, a neighborhood policing program might be introduced on an experimental basis. Matched pairs of police sectors would be identified, with the members of each pair being selected on the basis of similar population and crime characteristics. One member of each pair would then be selected at random (e.g., using a table of random numbers) to be part of the program.

If trends in the evaluation data before the new program is introduced are similar in both members of the pairs and the areas served by the program subsequently show marked improvement over the areas without the program, this provides considerable evidence for attributing the change to the program. Another example:

> A local government is considering installation of high intensity street lighting to combat neighborhood crime and reduce traffic accidents. Before spending large sums for this purpose, it decides to test whether the program will actually reduce crime and accidents. A number of geographical areas within the jurisdiction are identified that have similar characteristics (e.g., crime and accident rates, population density, traffic patterns, family income). Some of these areas are then randomly selected for installation of the new lighting. After a period of time—perhaps six months or a year—the crime and accident rates in the test and nontest areas are compared. Other plausible explanations for changes in the criteria, such as events that may have occurred in some areas and not in others, should be considered. If a significant reduction in crime and accidents has occurred in the areas with new street lighting and no other explanations are found, the changes can be attributed with some confidence to the new program. An expansion of the program to other areas would then seem appropriate. If there are no significant reductions in crime or accidents, on the other hand, expansion of the program may be a waste of resources.

Special Problems

For this fourth evaluation design, certain factors can make the observed results unrepresentative of the program's future effects. This possibility should be considered when the results of an evaluation using this design are examined.[18] Here are some examples of problems that can occur:

- The members of an experimental group may respond differently to a program if they realize they are being observed as part of the

---

18. References 4, 10, 13, 35, 36, and 37 contain excellent discussions of the types of problems encountered in this type of evaluation.

evaluation. This occurrence is commonly known as the "Hawthorne effect."

- If the experimental group is only one part of a jurisdiction, the response to a program may differ from what it would be if all parts of the jurisdiction were being served by the program. For example, crime control programs, if instituted in one part of a city, may merely cause criminal activity to shift to other locations. Crime in the experimental areas may show a marked decrease, but the jurisdiction as a whole may experience no change.

- If persons are allowed to volunteer for membership in the experimental group, the control and experimental groups are not likely to be comparable. A self-selected group will probably be more receptive to the program and thus may not be typical of the whole target population.

- In some situations, political pressures may make it impractical to provide a service to one group in the jurisdiction and not to others. This resistance will probably be less if the government tests a number of program variations instead of making an "all or nothing" allocation of resources.

- Similarly, concern about the equal distribution of services among population groups may limit the ability of governments to provide a service to one group while withholding the same service from another group. This problem will be less acute if there is a substantial question about whether the program is beneficial.[19]

- It may be considered morally wrong by some to provide a government service temporarily (during the experiment) when the service could cause clients to become dependent and make them worse off after the service is terminated. This problem may be partly overcome by explanations of the experiment in advance.

- The program must be controlled to make sure that experimental conditions are maintained—for example, that the intervention is maintained within the experimental group but is not introduced into the control group. In actual practice, how-

19. Reference 35 discusses the problem of program admission requirements. For example, if an existing law requires a government to admit to the program all who are qualified under the admission requirements, it may be impossible to find a satisfactory control group. If different treatments are being tested, however, random assignment to various treatment groups can be made.

ever, it is virtually impossible to control experimental conditions fully outside a laboratory. Since there will be some deviation from the intended implementation of the experiment, the evaluators will have to make adjustments or qualify their findings accordingly.

Cost

This design generally costs considerably more than other designs because of:

- the greater amount of time required to plan and conduct the experiment and to monitor the program procedures during the experimental period, and
- the higher level of analytical and administrative skills required for planning and undertaking the evaluation and analyzing the results.

This design also involves an indirect cost caused by temporary changes in the program to make sure that different programs are received by the experimental and the control groups.

Design Number 5: Comparisons of Planned vs. Actual Performance

In addition to comparisons of measurements from different time periods or for different groups, another type of comparison can also be useful. This is the comparison of actual results with planned or targeted results. Targets that are met or exceeded are evidence for maintaining or expanding the program. Conversely, targets that are not met raise questions about the program.

This is a fairly straightforward approach and perhaps should not be labeled a design. Preparation of plans for the next year is often done in state or local governments, although these plans are generally based on measures of workload and population served rather than on measurements of the effects of services. In addition, after-the-fact comparisons of how a program performed with what it had planned to do are still surprisingly rare.

The steps in this evaluation approach are as follows:

- Identify relevant objectives and corresponding evaluation criteria.
- Set specific goals or targets for these criteria for the specific time period.

- Obtain data after the time period on actual performance.
- Compare actual performance with the targets.
- Look for plausible explanations for changes in the values of the criteria other than the program. If there are any, estimate their effect on the criteria or at least identify them when presenting the findings.

Types of Application

This kind of evaluation can be undertaken if a government establishes targets that are expressed in terms of effectiveness measures. The targets should be stated in terms of specific achievements for specific time periods.

For example, the goal of a vocational rehabilitation program might be to rehabilitate a certain number of people in each disability category during the next year—for a given amount of resources. (The term "rehabilitate" will need to be defined as specifically as possible.)

This design, like Design Number 1, provides no direct means of indicating the extent to which changes in the values of the criteria can be attributed to the program. As with the other evaluation designs, evaluators should look for other plausible explanations as to why the targets have been met, exceeded, or not met. In the vocational rehabilitation example, for instance, there might have been a larger number of unusually difficult cases in a given disability category (that is, the type of clientele might have changed significantly).

This design can also be used to evaluate the performance of contractors if performance targets can be established for specific contracts.

> Charlotte, North Carolina, utilized this design to evaluate a variety of contracts. For example, for its In-School Career Employment Experience program it established a set of targets, including the number of youths who would receive work experience and training (to measure quantity), the number of positive terminations, that is, the number of youths who subsequently found employment or continued their education (to measure quality), and the proportion of participants in the targeted age and sex categories (to determine whether the clients served were part of the targeted population.)[20]

The example above provides an illustration of the essential weakness of this design. Even though the principal target (the number of

---

20. See Reference 58.

youths employed) may have been met, use of the design would not show whether the youths would have been employed if they had not participated in the program.

This evaluation approach can be used widely and regularly once provision is made for regular collection of the data needed. Setting targets each year for one year in advance can readily be done. Consequently, this design is particularly useful for annual evaluations of programs that have existed for a number of years (but where preprogram data may not be of much utility).

Special Problems

This approach requires the establishment of appropriate, realistic, and comprehensive targets. But such target setting may not be taken seriously if the evaluations are not used seriously.

If they are used seriously, the establishment of targets is likely to become an important issue. Higher-level officials as well as program managers should participate in setting targets. The targets should explicitly include all key program effects.

A major concern should be whether the targets are too easy, or too difficult, to achieve. This design assumes that the targets are the best available estimates of what actual accomplishments should be.

In establishing targets, agencies should consider the varying degrees of difficulty of the workload. In social services programs, for example, improvement rates for different types of clients will vary. Thus, separate targets should be set for each type of client in order to assess more accurately the effectiveness of the program.

Separate targets should also be established when the goal is to evaluate a program's efficiency, as the following example suggests:

> New York City's Office of Operations initially established a single daily target of 15.9 tons of garbage for each three-man truck for all the city's sanitation districts. At the urging of the Sanitation Department, however, the city established separate targets for the trucks in each sanitation district, based on the district's population density, distance from the dump, and types of parking restrictions.[21]

Another concern is that this design should not be used to encourage haphazard evaluations or to discourage the use of the tougher but more meaningful evaluation discussed earlier.

---

21. See Reference 67.

Cost

This design is likely to be the least expensive. The cost will depend primarily on the cost of collecting any additional data required for the evaluation criteria selected. The target-setting cost is likely to be small.

Additional Considerations for All Evaluation Designs

Program evaluators should take the following additional considerations into account:

Need to Separate Outcomes by Workload Characteristics

The workload of government agencies is typically more heterogeneous than it is homogeneous. There is likely to be considerable variation in the characteristics, and difficulty, of each request for agency action. Some examples:

- The existence of witnesses or the amount of evidence found at the scene of a crime can greatly affect the solving of a crime.
- Purchase orders for new and complex items are likely to require considerably more purchasing department effort than repeat, simpler, items.
- A particular program may work better for some clients (e.g., same age groups) than others.
- Eligibility application forms can differ significantly in complexity and thus require significantly different procedures or amount of effort by agency employees.
- It will be easier to find adoptive placements for healthy babies than for older, problem children.
- Terrain and soil conditions can significantly affect both the costs of road maintenance and the quality and duration of road repairs.
- The quality of the water coming into a water treatment plant will affect the plant's costs to remove impurities and probably the quality of the effluent.

Therefore, the incoming workload should be classified into categories; each category should represent a potentially different degree of difficulty for the service. Program outcomes should subsequently be assessed for each category, and not only for the total aggregate workload. This serves two purposes:[22]

---

22. A third purpose for these breakouts, to help suggest program improvements, will be discussed in Chapter 5.

1. Some programs may be effective in serving one type of work-load (e.g., older clients or one type of road surface) but be less effective in serving other types. Providing outcome information for each type will, thus, give officials a better perspective on the program's effectiveness, that is, it will indicate for which workload the program is effective and for which it is not.

2. The reason for apparent aggregate, poor performance (or good performance) of a program could be the mix of the incoming workload. A breakout by category will reveal this.

This second purpose is somewhat subtle and warrants further clarification. For Evaluation Designs 1, 2, and 5, the mix of the workload might change over time—to a more difficult, or easier, mix. For Designs 3 and 4, the workload for the comparison group could be substantially more (or less) difficult than the workload for the group receiving the program. (Random assignment of the work-load in Design Number 4 is intended to reduce the likelihood that such differences would occur; however, even with correct random assignment procedures, there is the possibility that differences will occur.) Thus, breaking out the outcomes by these various categories of workload will permit officials to avoid interpreting a difference in the mix of workload as a real difference in program effectiveness. This can be illustrated by the following example:

	1979	1980
Total Clients	500	500
Total Helped	300	235
Percent	60%	47%
Severe Cases		
Total Number	100	300
Total Helped	0	75
Percent	0%	25%
Non-Severe Cases		
Total Number	400	200
Total Helped	300	160
Percent	75%	80%

If only the total aggregate data are examined, it appears that program performance has deteriorated. However, if the breakouts by category of workload are examined, the figures indicate that the program actually performed better on each type of workload. What happened is that the mix of workload changed significantly, with a greater portion of more difficult workload occurring in the second year. Breaking out the outcome data has helped avoid what otherwise could have been a gross misinterpretation of the effectiveness of the program.

Seldom Can One Be Absolutely Certain that a Change Was Brought About by a Specific Program.

Almost always, there is some chance that other factors caused the change. Even in controlled experiments (Design Number 4), it is not feasible to control for all the factors that may affect outcomes, in addition to the program itself.

> During one period in Washington, D.C., for example, there was a drop in the reported crime rate. Several major changes had occurred during the period, including major increases in the number of police officers, expansion of a drug addict treatment program, and extensive new street lighting in some portions of the city. In addition, some observers believed that social conditions had changed significantly in the city during the time period. The effects of some of these changes on the reported crime rate could have been at least partially isolated—e.g., the street lighting effects presumably would occur only in areas where the lighting was added, but the effect of other factors would have been difficult, if not impossible, to isolate.

But even when it is not possible to isolate the effects of one program from other programs introduced about the same time, an evaluation that indicates that the community is receiving significant benefits is worthwhile. It at least suggests to government officials that there is no need to break up a winning combination.

Can Projections Be Made from the Evaluation's Findings?

The purpose of evaluation is to help guide future government actions. Even where the evaluation indicates with considerable certainty that a program has had a significant effect in the past, some circumstances can make it hazardous to predict that the program will have similar effects in the future. These circumstances include such situations as the following:

- If only a part of a program is evaluated, the findings may not be applicable to full-scale implementation.
- If special personnel or special equipment are used in the program being tested but are not available in the post-test period or for a full-scale implementation, the degree of success due to these special capabilities may not be obtainable in the future.

Were Only Short-Term Effects Measured?

A program that appears successful over a short term may begin to cause new problems over the long run (e.g., ground water pollution in a solid waste disposal landfill, sideeffects from prolonged use of special drugs to combat illnesses, etc.). Or the observed effects of a program may disappear as clients or personnel become used to the new intervention—in effect, the new procedure becomes commonplace. Problems of this type are a good reason for requiring periodic follow-up.

Exhibit 12 illustrates the potential danger of not having a long enough time period after implementation on which to base an evaluation.

> The effect of the Connecticut program on the fatality rate for the first year after program implementation (1956) gave little indication of the program's long-run consequences. The reduction in the fatality rate from 1955 to 1956 might have occurred anyway, or the drop may have been large only because of the large (perhaps random) jump in fatalities in 1955. Only in 1957 did the time series begin to show a significantly different pattern than that which existed before 1956[23]

State and local governments, however, often cannot wait long periods of time before making decisions about future program activities. Where decisions cannot be delayed, intermediate findings should be provided. However, the problems that make it difficult to interpret such findings should be clearly explained to government officials.

Where Possible, Collect Data on the Evaluation Criteria before Program Implementation Rather Than Relying on After-the-Fact Reconstruction of the Data.

The first three designs can be used even after a program has been operating for a period of time if adequate data on preprogram condi-

---

23. This and similar problems are discussed in Reference 9.

tions are available or can be reconstructed. In practice, the majority of state and local evaluations are done after the fact. This, however, greatly restricts the evaluation criteria that can be used, since often desirable data on conditions before the new program is introduced cannot be obtained. Normally, agencies collect little data on service effectiveness—for example, data on client satisfaction with public services (such as recreation, libraries, or public transit), or on the amount of client improvement after clients receive health or social services. As a result, after-the-fact evaluations often have to rely on other information, such as counts of clients, that say little about the quality of the service.

Agencies with outcome monitoring systems will be able to rely on after-the-fact evaluations more frequently because preimplementation data for some programs will be routinely available.

Choice of an Evaluation Design

Selecting an evaluation design depends on when the evaluation is to be conducted, the dollars available, and the degree of accuracy desired.

The first four designs are progressively more expensive, with the fourth usually (but not always) considerably more expensive than the others. The first three and the fifth can often be accomplished with only a few staff-months of analytical effort, with the amount of time required depending on how much effort is required to collect data not normally collected. The fourth design is likely to take many months and possibly years. It could well take several staff-years of special effort to design, monitor, and analyze the findings.

The first four designs are also progressively more effective in providing accurate evaluation information, the fourth usually providing by far the best evidence as to the effects of the program.

The designs are not either/or choices. Some or all of the first three are often used together.

Recommendations

1. Whenever practical, utilize the most precise evaluation design, which is Design Number 4. "One conclusive evaluation can be much less costly than several inconclusive studies using other designs."[24] However, its cost and special characteristics mean that a local government should probably use Design 4 very

---

24. See Reference 61, p. 5.

selectively. State governments will probably be able to use this design more often, since they often have more resources and, sometimes, longer-term time horizons than local governments; and use of the design can be justified on grounds that state programs have wider application. The use of geographical areas as control groups should be explored by both state and local governments.

2. When it is not feasible to use Design 4, use Designs 1, 2, and 3 in combination. That is, the evaluation should look at before and after values for the criteria, undertake projections for selected criteria where prior-year data are available, and search for similar population segments that have not been served by the program. The findings from the use of all three designs should be utilized in drawing conclusions. The additional cost of using Designs 2 and 3 in tandem with Design Number 1 should, in general, not be great, and the added meaningfulness of the evaluation should be well worth the added cost.

3. Avoid using Design Number 1 by itself except as a last resort. Evaluation Design Number 1 is not a strong evaluation tool.

4. Make regular use of Design Number 5—setting targets for individual evaluation criteria. This design, however, should be considered a supplement to the other designs.

5. Whatever the design initially chosen, it should be altered or changed if subsequent events provide good reason to do so. In some cases, a design will have to be altered because additional evaluation criteria are found to be necessary after the evaluation begins. In other cases, a different design may have to be substituted for the original one (for example, when a controlled experiment becomes contaminated by unwanted deviations from the original plan for the experiment). The evaluators will, however, need to make a good case for any changes so that they are not accused of manipulating the evaluation.

Special Note on Outcome Monitoring

Chapter 1 suggests that monitoring of outcomes to provide annual feedback on major programs and services should be a regular practice, along with in-depth evaluations of individual programs.[25] Reg-

---

25. Our observation is that most of what is currently labeled program evaluation in state and local governments is little more than outcome monitoring done irregularly. Many evaluations are of short duration and merely take snapshots of the current values of selected evaluation criteria.

ular feedback is desirable for such purposes as budgeting, program planning and motivating employees. Such monitoring can take on the characteristics of some of the evaluation designs described in this chapter. Data on outcomes collected over time, for example, will provide time series data. The regularly collected data can sometimes be used to compare preprogram and postprogram outcomes. If outcome data are disaggregated by geographical area (e.g., county, neighborhood, service district, facility) or by individual programs that have similar objectives, the resulting data can provide (crude) comparison group information.

Analyzing regularly collected outcome data is no substitute for an in-depth look at a specific program, however. A special, in-depth evaluation can be tailored much more carefully to a specific program and set of circumstances, as, for example, to look for other plausible explanations for the observed outcomes.

IV. THE DIRTY JOB—DATA COLLECTION

Collecting data is often considered a mechanical task and the least interesting part of program evaluation. However, it probably consumes the greatest amount of time and effort.

This chapter focuses on the major factors in data collection that should be of most concern to program evaluation.

Most of the discussion applies equally to data collected for regular outcome monitoring and to individual program evaluations. Regular outcome monitoring requires the establishment of standard procedures so that data are collected routinely and are comparable from one year to the next. Individual program evaluations may require tailor-made data collection procedures that may not be feasible on a regular basis.[1]

The data to be collected are determined in large part by the evaluation criteria, client groups, and evaluation design that are selected. Identification of relevant clientele groups will suggest the type of data disaggregation that will be needed (see Chapter 2). The specific time periods or the specific groups for which data are required will be dictated by the selection of the evaluation design (see Chapter 3).

The data used in an evaluation must have three characteristics: (1) they should be reasonably accurate; (2) they should be reasonably complete; and (3) since evaluation relies on comparisons of data collected at different times, and possibly for different population segments, they should be comparable.

Many problems relating to the accuracy, completeness, and comparability of data can be avoided if the evaluation is planned before program implementation so the same data collection procedures are used for both periods. Preplanned evaluations have another advantage. Often, the data needed for a thorough evaluation are not normally routinely collected by government agencies. Thus, data for particular evaluation criteria (such as client satisfaction with the

---

1. Individual program evaluations can also provide the framework for an ongoing system of data collection. Once procedures for collecting data on the evaluation criteria have been developed and tested, those procedures could be adapted for regular outcome monitoring.

57

service) will not be available for the period before the new program. Through preplanning, provision can be made to collect relevant data both before and after implementation.

There are five principal sources of data:

- Existing records and statistics.
- Feedback from the program's clientele, which in some cases will be the general population (e.g., crime and fire protection services) and in others will be small sub-sets of the population (e.g., mental health programs).
- Ratings by trained observers.
- Other special data collection procedures.
- The experience of other governments.

Existing Records and Statistics

A certain amount of data are routinely collected on every government program, and some of these data can be useful in an evaluation. For example, an evaluation of police effectiveness will probably require police department records on the numbers of crimes and arrests, and possibly data from the prosecutor's office and the courts on the subsequent disposition of the arrests.

Often, however, current statistics based on the data will be inadequate, and it will be necessary to check basic records to obtain the needed information. For example, in the evaluation of the Dade County, Florida, drug user treatment program, it was necessary to determine the addresses of drug addicts in order to evaluate the degree to which (based on the geographic distribution of counseling and treatment services) the services were accessible to the clients. A special review of addict records was needed to collect their addresses.[2]

Although records of complaints are often kept, complaints often are not tabulated according to subject matter. Information on the disposition of complaints—such as the amount of time required to resolve them—also is rare.

Data about program costs are another type of information that generally must be obtained by a special review of program records. (Cost analysis is discussed later in this chapter.)

A special problem occurs in those program evaluations in which it is necessary to track the history of individual clients from their entry into the governmental system (data on reasons for entry, per-

---

2. Reference 57.

sonal characteristics of clients, intermediate dispositions of clients) through ultimate disposition (such as reason for departure and whether the client had to return subsequently for further treatment). This need usually occurs in evaluations of treatment or correction programs. In some situations, one agency's information on specific individuals may have to be linked with records on the same individuals in other agencies. When done for a number of individuals, such information can be aggregated to relate disposition and treatment success to reasons for entry and client characteristics.

> The Nashville, Tennessee, evaluation of existing programs for short-term care of neglected children, for example, needed to obtain data on the characteristics of the children at intake from welfare agencies, data on length of stay at the Children's Home from that institution, and data on subsequent disposition from the juvenile court and other agencies. Linking was necessary to relate the reason for entry to type of disposition for each individual child.[3]

> The Dade County drug abuse program evaluation linked information from individual treatment programs to jail and arrest records. This was necessary to determine whether the long-term success of certain types of treatment varied according to treatment or to a client's personal characteristics, such as age, length of time on drugs, and educational level.[4]

Existing records are seldom sufficient by themselves for a program evaluation. As already noted, information on key program effects is often not available. In the evaluation of Operation Clean Sweep, for example, data were not available on street cleanliness or on citizen perceptions of litter conditions, odors from garbage, and noise during collections. Such data therefore had to be gathered from other sources.

Evaulators must watch for changes, or differences, in procedures or definitions of data categories. This is especially important when comparing data from many different time periods or jurisdictions. In such cases, if appropriate adjustments are not or cannot be made, the data are likely to be inconsistent.

---

3. Reference 56.

4. Reference 57.

Feedback from Clients

Feedback from clients of government services will, in many cases, be a major way of obtaining information on program effectiveness. Three types of uses are as follows:[5]

- To determine the condition of individuals after they leave government-sponsored programs. For some programs (such as health, drug, alcoholism, and job training), follow-up is likely to be needed to determine the condition of individuals after they have left a particular program. Because few records are usually available on clients after they leave a government treatment program, there is little basis for judging the program's long-term effectiveness. Locating and interviewing former participants (as was done in the Dade County drug treatment program study) may be the only practical way to obtain information on their current condition.[6]

- To assess citizen satisfaction with services. Most residents of a jurisdiction are potential users of basic government services, such as solid waste collection, crime control, recreation, transportation, etc. An important factor in assessing the quality of these services is the perception of citizens about their adequacy.[7]

- To obtain certain factual data. Surveys can, and have been, used to gather information on such elements as how many different persons use, or do not use, government-provided facilities or programs, the frequency of missed garbage collections, the frequency of rodent sightings, their current employment status, etc.

---

5. References 24 (Chapter 14), 27, 47, and 50 discuss the use of, and procedures for, citizen surveys for state and local governments. References 3, 29, and 45 provide additional information on survey procedures.

6. Examples of surveys of persons known to have been clients of a specific program can be found in References 24 (for a number of municipal services), 25 (social services), and 39 (mental health).

7. Citizen surveys also provide diagnostic information (that is, clues) about what is deficient in government programs. Citizens can be asked, for example, why they do not use recreational or public transit facilities. Citizens who do use them can be asked for their views on specific matters, such as safety, hours of operation, accessibility, cleanliness, and so on. Information of this kind can be quite helpful in providing guidance on how to improve services. (See Chapter 5 for further discussion of this.)

Client feedback can be used in both individual program evaluations and for outcome monitoring of major program areas. As part of their regular monitoring of outcomes, state and local governments should conduct annual surveys of citizens covering a variety of evaluation criteria for a variety of major programs. Individual program evaluations may be able to use some of the results from these surveys. In other instances, individual program evaluations may require data from clients not normally included in an annual outcome monitoring survey or may have to be conducted at some other time than the regular survey.

If a government does not undertake regular surveys—and few currently do—special surveys for program evaluation may be needed.[8]

Means of Collection

Interviews with haphazardly selected samples, it should be noted, can produce misleading results. Mailed questionnaires, for instance, more than one mode of administering the questionnaire. Mailings supplemented by telephone or in-person interviews, or telephone surveys supplemented by in-person interviews, can be used. These surveys use the more expensive mode only for those in the sample not responding to the less expensive approach.

When the group to be interviewed is large, it is often very costly to attempt to interview every member of the group. Instead, interviews of a representative sample of the group are used to provide representative data.

Interviews with haphazardly selected samples, it should be noted, can produce misleading results. Mailed questionnaires, for instance, are likely to be an inaccurate way to measure citizen attitudes because of the self-selective nature of the response—if special effort is not undertaken to obtain reasonable response rates.

If a sample is properly selected and the rate of response is good (i.e., 50 to 60 percent or better), the responses are more likely to be representative of the group as a whole. Surveys of several hundred citizens are likely to provide sufficiently precise results for most purposes, even in large jurisdictions. (The Gallup and Harris polls typically use samples of about 1,600 to represent the whole coun-

---

8. Jurisdictions that have used citizen surveys on a regular basis for outcome monitoring include Dallas, Texas; Dayton, Ohio; Kansas City, Missouri; Randolph Township, New Jersey; and St. Petersburg, Florida.

try.) As few as 100 respondents may be adequate to provide sufficiently accurate results on particular client groups.

The surveys should also obtain information on relevant demographic characteristics (such as location of residents, age group, race, sex, etc.) to permit the comparison of service outcomes for different clientele groups.

Limitations

There are a number of limitations to the use of surveys of clients:

First, there is considerable time and cost involved. However, the growing acceptability of the telephone survey and combinations of modes is making surveys more economical. A sample composed of 600 telephone interviews (of 20 minutes each) may cost $10,000 or less. If appropriate in-house or volunteer workers are available it may be possible to reduce the cost further.

Second, special techniques are needed to design survey procedures and the questionnaire to be used. The questions should be carefully worded and then tested to make sure that they do not elicit ambiguous or misleading responses. The selection of persons to be interviewed must also be done carefully to avoid introducing bias into the results. In some cases, such as follow-up interviews with persons no longer enrolled in treatment programs, it may be difficult to locate the persons to be interviewed.

Third, unless a survey is conducted before program implementation—to be compared with the results of a survey taken after implementation and using the same wording—a direct before vs. after comparison will not be possible. This problem can be partly circumvented by asking respondents to compare their current situation (e.g., the cleanliness of their street) with their situation, say, a year ago (before program implementation). This approach, however, may put excessive reliance on the memory of the respondents.

Fourth, survey information is limited by the respondent's memory and willingness to answer candidly.

Fifth, some persons may refuse to be interviewed perhaps regarding the interview as an invasion of privacy; at times this may prevent obtaining an adequate sample. This problem frequently can be alleviated, however, if the interviewers are properly trained.

Ratings by Trained Observers

In some situations, ratings by trained observers may be appropriate for evaluating program effects. When used, such ratings should be output-oriented and conducted systematically.

Trained observers have been used to assess, among other things, the cleanliness of streets, the "rideability" of roads, the condition of housing, the physical condition of institutions (such as residential homes for the aged and corrections facilities), the quality of park maintenance, and the condition of clients of mental health and social services.[9]

Means of Collection

Some form of prespecified, standardized rating scale should be established, with explicit directions provided for using each reading on the scale. The raters should be adequately trained to use the rating procedures. The rating system should be such that different observers, observing the same conditions at different times, give approximately the same rating. A pretest is highly desirable to see if different observers using the specified procedures give reasonably similar ratings.

> An example is the special rating system that was used in Washington, D.C.'s Operation Clean Sweep program for measuring the cleanliness of streets. A scale using a number of photographs, each representing one of four grades of cleanliness, was prepared. Thus, different inspectors at different periods of time inspecting different parts of the jurisdiction had standards (the photographs) against which to make their judgments.[10]

Ratings can be made of all streets, houses, clients, and so on, or if this is not practical, of a random sample.

---

9. See, for example, References 2 (mental health), 5 (street cleanliness), 20 (road smoothness), 24 (street cleanliness and road smoothness), 32 (road smoothness), and 67 (street cleanliness).

10. The photographs and the scale itself were selected by a group of "judges," who separated a large group of photographs, covering many types of conditions, into four grades. If the judges could not agree on the grade for a particular photograph, it was excluded. Thus, the final sixteen photographs (four for each grade) and the resulting scale represented a high consensus of opinion. The judges were not professionals but a cross section of citizens. See Reference 5 for further details. This procedure has also been used by New York City's Department of Sanitation. See Reference 67.

Finally, raters should be selected who do not have a self-interest in the outcome. It is not appropriate that the individuals who give the service also provide the effectiveness ratings.

> In another case, professional social workers were used to assess family functioning at different times. The social workers were given instructions on the aspects of family functioning to be rated. Each aspect was rated according to a standard descriptive scale. The quality of sibling relationships, for example, was assessed on the basis of criteria for each grade on the scale:[11]
>
> Inadequate: There is conflict between children resulting in physical violence or cruelty which warrants intervention . . .
>
> Marginal: Emotional ties among children weak . . . rarely play together . . .
>
> Adequate: Positive emotional ties and mutual identification . . .
>
> The ratings were made by firsthand observation of the family.

Limitations

This method will be of limited value without observers who have been adequately trained to make the ratings and who can be objective in their appraisals. Furthermore, considerable time and effort using appropriate expertise will be needed to establish an acceptable rating system if one is not already available.

The costs of this method may be large because of the time required for each observation and the specialized personnel involved. However, if such ratings can be made by employed personnel as part of their regular jobs, or by (properly trained) volunteers or interns, the out-of-pocket costs to a government may be small.

Another problem is that, as time passes, raters may unknowingly deviate from the rating scale. Periodic analyses of ratings and retraining in the use of the scale are needed to prevent this. In one case, checks of ratings by inspectors who were using the street cleanliness rating scales indicated that after a period of time the inspectors tended to compress the scale, i.e., to give fewer extreme ratings. As a result, the inspectors were retrained in using the scale.

This method of data collection is somewhat subjective and preferably should be used in conjunction with more objective measurements. For example, professional ratings of child adjustment might be supplemented by reports of difficulties experienced by the child in school.

---

11. See Reference 19.

Other Special Data Collection Procedures

As already indicated, most evaluations are likely to require some data not currently available. Other procedures for the collection of these data may be needed.

The methods that can be used are limited only by the ingenuity of the evaluators. They may involve systematic field observations, such as speed and delay on major traffic arteries, or special counts of participants in recreational activities. Another example:

> An evaluation of road maintenance in Fairfax County, Virginia, to assess whether one particular area of the county was at the same rideability level as the rest of the county, was made with a mechanical device called the roughometer. The device gathered data on inches of roughness per mile as an indicator of the comfortableness of the ride.[12] (Many state governments are using this type of device for periodic assessments of road condition.)

Another approach might be called special event or scenario analysis. This applies to unusual events on which information normally is not collected. Examples are the use of helicopters to apprehend suspects, the use of on-line communications to allow police officers in the field to identify wanted persons or stolen automobiles, and consolidation of police or fire services.

The data are collected on particular events to indicate the degree to which the program was useful or not, e.g., the degree to which the police helicopter actually helped in making an arrest. The frequency of each type of event is then estimated. The data can be collected by developing a special (temporary) reporting form if the evaluation is preplanned. Otherwise, such information must be reconstructed from the memories of the persons involved.

A related approach, labeled the critical incident technique, attempts to identify the number and type of critical incidents. In psychiatric treatment, for example, the evaluators might seek to identify what a patient can do after treatment that he could not do before.

Some precautions pertinent to the collection methods described previously are worth noting again. Procedures for collecting data should be standardized, regardless of whether the data are subjective ratings or direct measurements. Factors that should be standardized include (a) the criteria for selecting observation points, (b) the factors

---

12. The analysis of the condition of different roads is described in Reference 6. References 20, 24 (Chapter 8), and 32 also discuss this type of measurement procedure.

to be measured or noted, and (c) the procedures for operating the measurement device or gathering the subjective data. The measurement of road quality by the roughometer, for example, was standardized for such factors as weather conditions and vehicle type and speed.

Limitations

Procedures for the collection of special data invariably entail added cost. As with the other data collection methods described earlier, however, costs can often be reduced by sampling rather than attempting to count all possible observations. If proper sampling procedures are used, sufficient accuracy can usually be obtained. Using the roughometer to test the condition of all the roads in Fairfax County, for example, would have been too expensive. All the roads in the smaller area were tested, but only a sample of roads was tested in the larger area.[13]

The Experience of Other Governments

Information on the experience of other governments will sometimes be useful for evaluation. This will particularly be the case with Design 3 where other jurisdictions are used as comparison groups. On-site visits probably will be needed, however, to screen out general information of a public-relations type and to attempt to obtain comparable data.

Unfortunately, there are likely to be major deficiencies in the available data, including desired data that are not collected at all, data that are collected but using different procedures or different definitions, and the existence of external factors in the other jurisdiction that affect the comparability of the data (such as significantly different clientele characteristics).

Need for Multiple Data Collection Procedures

In most evaluations it is necessary to use more than one data collection procedure. Generally, data will be sought for more than one criterion, but even when only one criterion is used it may be desirable to use multiple sources to provide corroboration.

- To evaluate its hot meals program for the aged, Charlotte, North Carolina, used:

---

13. See Reference 6.

(a) agency records to obtain counts of the number of persons served each day,

(b) interviews with program participants at the meal sites about the quality of the meals, and

(c) ratings of evaluation office staff and others who acted as trained observers, eating with program participants and rating the quality of the meals and the social atmosphere. The observers rated the food as to taste, temperature, appearance, texture, and nutritional value. One group of trained observers were the ministers of the five churches at which the meals were provided. They provided ratings of the quality of the food served, the catering service used, and the entertainment programs held in association with the meals.[14]

- To evaluate the accessibility of its welfare centers, San Diego County used:

(a) department records on the location of welfare clients,

(b) census statistics on the location of low-income families,

(c) interviews with welfare clients and prospective clients on how they reach the centers and how they rated the accessibility of these centers,

(d) information on bus schedules to determine accessibility by bus, and

(e) department records on operating costs to help determine the optimal size of the centers.[15]

Multi-Agency Problems

In those fortunate cases where data from only a single agency within the government are required for an evaluation, there may not be many collection problems. However, in more complex evaluations, data will generally be required from more than one government agency and often from agencies or groups outside the government as well.

Data may be required from many sources: government agencies associated with the program, other governments in other locations (when used as comparison groups—see Chapter 3), other layers of government affecting the jurisdiction, private agencies, and indi-

---

14. Reference 59.

15. Reference 77.

viduals in the community. An evaluation of a city's drug treatment programs, for example, would need the following: data from the records of each treatment program, some of which may be privately operated; information from the medical examiner on deaths apparently due to drug use; information from police and court agencies on drug-related arrests and convictions; information from the corrections department on the number of addicted persons put in prisons or jail; information from the health department on drug-related illnesses; possibly, information from county and state welfare agencies to identify changes in the ability of past drug users to support themselves and their families; information directly from clients who have dropped out or graduated; and information from addicts who, though never enrolled in a treatment program, act as a comparison group.

Obtaining information from agencies within a government is often difficult enough, but obtaining it from agencies outside the government can really be a challenge. Government officials often must help the evaluation team surmount this obstacle, and skill in external relations will be important.

The Confidentiality Issue

Some program evaluations will require data on individual citizens. It is neither necessary nor appropriate to present data on specific individuals in evaluation reports. The information presented in the findings should be aggregated and mask individual identities. Nevertheless, questions on confidentiality are bound to be raised when the records of individual clients are used.[16] It is the obligation of the government to ensure that confidentiality is maintained. It is never appropriate to show data that permit identification of specific individuals. Adequate steps are needed to assure that the information obtained on individuals will be safeguarded and used only in aggregate summaries. Documents with individual names should be handled by a minimum number of carefully selected persons. Numerical coding on intermediate tabulations is another safeguard that should be used.

In addition, no citizens or clients should be required to answer questions on their personal lives solely for evaluation purposes. And, especially where there may be some health or safety hazard

---

16. Legal issues as well as ethical ones are involved. See Reference 35 for further discussion of this problem.

involved, their participation in an experiment (Evaluation Design 4) should require clients' informed consent. In most cases, however, clients' participation in an experiment or filling out evaluation questionnaires is not likely to involve a significant intrusion on their privacy or be harmful. With proper explanation to clients, most will cooperate.

However, it is important that state and local governments remember that programs supported by public funds, whether actually undertaken by public or private agencies, should be required to provide data needed to help assess whether a jurisdiction is using its resources wisely.

Private agencies that are either directly supported by, or regulated by, the government should, where appropriate, be required to provide the information needed to evaluate the quality and effectiveness as well as cost of the service they provide. In some cases, this may mean added costs to the private agency, and—as with agencies inside the government—the contracting government should provide reasonable funding for data collection. Both the public and private agency should follow confidentiality safeguards such as those noted above.

Cost Analysis

Program cost analysis is itself a topic worthy of extensive discussion, but only a few elements of major concern to the sponsors and users of program evaluation are singled out here.[17]

One of the major problems in every evaluation is to make sure that the cost estimates for the program include all relevant costs. A checklist of cost elements should be prepared for a program being evaluated. A generalized list of such cost elements is provided in Exhibit 14. However, more detailed checklists for each type of service should be quite useful to governments that regularly conduct evaluations.

---

17. This section addresses only monetary costs. The term "costs" is often used in a broader sense to refer to all of the negative effects of a program. Negative nonmonetary costs should be covered by other evaluation criteria, however, and we do not encourage the imputation of monetary values to all evaluation criteria, as is sometimes proposed to permit the calculation of cost-benefit ratios. Existing procedures for assigning monetary values to nonmonetary criteria involve too many value judgments to be of major use to state and local government managers.

Exhibit 14.   ELEMENTS OF PROGRAM COST

1. One-time, fixed costs
   Planning, development, engineering
   Test and evaluation

2. Investment costs
   Land
   Building and facilities
   Equipment and vehicles
   Initial training

3. Recurring costs (operating and maintenance costs)
   Personnel salaries, wages, and fringe benefits for direct operations
   Maintenance of equipment, vehicles, and buildings
   Replacement and recurring training costs
   Direct contributions and payments to citizens, e.g., welfare pay-
      ments to the needy
   Payments to extra-governmental institutions for services for citi-
      zens; e.g., payments to agencies for foster home services
   Fuel costs
   Miscellaneous materials and supplies
   Miscellaneous support (overhead) costs

Source: Adapted from Reference 42.

Cost elements often omitted include the following:

- The costs of fringe benefits for the employees associated with the program.
- The costs incurred by a centralized garage for vehicle maintenance.
- Possible costs of using public land, public buildings, and other public facilities which, though they seem free to the program, incur some additional but hidden cost (for example, where rental income is lost because of the program's use of the facilities).

It may be difficult to extract from government cost accounting systems the actual costs of the programs being evaluated. In the Indianapolis Take-Home Car Plan, for example, the differences in per vehicle maintenance and fuel costs were very difficult to distinguish because no provision had been made for separating the costs incurred for police cars given to officers twenty-four hours a day from those that were not.

The ultimate purpose of cost estimates is to indicate likely future costs if a program is continued at either the same, an increased, or a reduced, level. Therefore, one-time costs that will not be incurred again should be distinguished.

The problem of how to determine related support and overhead cost is well known, but few satisfactory procedures exist. The major question is what the impact of the program being evaluated has been (and will continue to be) on such costs. The added cost to the government may be nil. However, if support activities and facilities were already working at or near capacity prior to the program, a new program could increase support costs significantly. A police take-home car plan, for example, might cause a change in maintenance needs and alter the need for garage facilities, equipment, and other garage costs.

In general, information on costs will be found in government records. But, as already indicated, there will be many gaps in the records. Special analysis of cost data will probably be needed to provide the cost estimates needed for individual, in-depth, program evaluations.

V. GETTING MORE FOR THE EVALUATION DOLLAR: USING EVALUATION TO IMPROVE THE PROGRAM

The first purpose of an evaluation is to assess the effectiveness of a program and thus to help determine whether it should be continued, expanded, cut back, or dropped. The question is: "How effective has the program been?"

But most, if not all, state and local government evaluations should also have a second purpose: to find ways to improve the program evaluated. The question here is: "What can be done to strengthen the program's future performance?"

Literature on program evaluation sometimes labels the first purpose as "summative" and the second as "formative." Sometimes, the literature implies that a program evaluation must have only one purpose. This book takes the position that state and local government evaluations should serve both purposes.

Using evaluation to identify potential program improvements is a good way of making it more attractive to program managers. Without their interest, program evaluation is likely to have to struggle continuously for its life.[1]

---

1. As indicated in Chapter 1, many, if not most, state and local governments conduct occasional examinations of the operation of their programs for the purpose of improving them. These are sometimes called management analyses, process evaluations, or some other term. It is not within the scope of this book to discuss procedures for assessing internal agency operations. However, the line between program evaluation (in which program impacts are scrutinized) and process evaluation (in which internal program procedures are studied) is often blurred. This overlap occurs when an evaluation that focuses on outcome is also used to provide information on processes, or when a process evaluation includes an examination of outcomes. Process evaluation can be combined with program evaluation to assure that the overall evaluation provides suggestions for program improvements. Or process evaluations can be triggered by a program evaluation whose findings suggest that substantial program improvements are needed. There are numerous techniques for process evaluation, including charting the work flow, performing critical-path analyses of work flow tasks, timing individual tasks, analyzing rates of error, surveying the staff at work, simulating both the work flow and proposed changes to the work flow with computer models, and a variety of work measure-

73

This chapter suggests four procedures to include in a program evaluation to help identify ways to improve the program evaluated. They are:

1. Examine the relationship between program outcomes and selected characteristics of the workload to identify the need for program variations for various classes of the workload.
2. Examine the relationship between program outcomes and the program's major operational characteristics to identify characteristics associated with favorable outcomes.
3. Obtain data on reasons for poor outcomes along with the outcome information.
4. Seek qualitative information on program problems during the course of the evaluation.

The first three tasks seek clues to program improvements by examining information on outcomes. The fourth is purely a process evaluation activity but is included here in the belief that program evaluators, who are already studying the program in depth, should not lose the golden opportunity offered by their investigation to provide program managers with potentially useful insights. Each of the four tasks is discussed below.

Examining the Relationship between Program Outcomes and Selected Characteristics of the Workload

As pointed out in Chapter 3, the workload that comes into a government agency each day is typically heterogeneous. This applies whether the incoming workload is in the form of clients, roads to be repaired, water to be treated, applications or orders to be processed, or whatever. There is likely to be considerable variation in the characteristics, and difficulty, of each request for agency action.

Given the inevitability of variations in the workload, it is usually desirable to devise different programs or procedures to deal with these variations. The issue here is whether evaluation data can be used to help identify what kind of program or procedural changes are needed.

Chapter 3 recommended that program outcomes for specific types of program clients, or other units of workload, of varying degrees of

---

ment and work simplification techniques. For an excellent discussion of the issues involved including process questions in program evaluations, see Reference 33, especially Chapter 8. References 1 and 30 also discuss these issues.

difficulty be collected. The reason for collecting such information was to help determine whether the program was more successful for certain types of workloads (clients) than for others and to avoid misinterpreting differences in the mix of the workload as differences in program effectiveness.

This same information can also provide clues on how the program might be improved. *The general principle is that information relating outcomes to client or other workload groupings can indicate whether the program needs to be adjusted for certain types of workloads (clients).*

If it is found, for example, that a health program is not effective for some types of clients, the methods used for treating those types of clients should be reviewed. This review may suggest possible modifications of the program, or, at the extreme, dropping of the program for those types of clients. For example, if a certain road maintenance procedure leads to substantially more enduring road surfaces and less costly maintenance for certain types of terrain than for others, different maintenance procedures should be considered for these others. If existing approaches to placing children for adoption are found to have poor success for certain kinds of children, different approaches might be considered for those children. The following is an example of how analysis of workload led to suggestions for possible program improvement:

> As part of a budget review, the city of Phoenix, Arizona, conducted an evaluation of its police department's new system of assigning some patrol cars to emergency-only duty. Response time to emergency calls was used as the principal evaluation criterion. Response times were calculated for each shift and each day of the week because the timing of demand was felt to be an important workload characteristic. After finding that response times were longer for the second shift than for other shifts regardless of the day of the week, the evaluators recommended increasing the number of emergency-only cars assigned to the second shift.[2]

Sometimes evaluators may not be able to identify some important workload (client) characteristics until the evaluation has been going on for some time. Evaluations should be planned so that, if important characteristics do appear during the evaluation, data can be collected on them and outcomes related to them. For example, if differences in terrain or soil conditions are identified as an impor-

---

2. Reference 75.

tant factor midway through an evaluation of a road maintenance program, road segments would then be classified by terrain and soil conditions. Data on duration of repair, road condition, and repair cost per mile would be obtained for each terrain or soil condition category.

It is preferable, of course, to identify significant workload (client) characteristics at the time the evaluation is being designed so that data collection and analysis can be scheduled more efficiently. If possible, the design should include comparison groups for each significant workload (client) characteristic. Even when this cannot be done, however, an examination of performance relative to the workload (client) characteristics should be undertaken in order to provide agency management with insights into program needs. In other words, the relationship between outcomes and workload characteristics should be systematically examined even if it cannot be controlled in the evaluation.

Examining the Relationship between Program Outcomes and the Program's Major Operational Characteristics

Sometimes programs are operated in a variety of ways, especially if they are operated in more than one location. Sometimes variations are introduced intentionally, in which case the evaluation should be designed from the outset to assess how the variations relate to outcomes. (See Evaluation Designs 3 and 4 in Chapter 3.) Even if the goal is to implement the same program at each location, however, there will inevitably be variations. Different offices, facilities, service delivery districts, precincts, fire stations, counties, etc., will inevitably operate a program in different ways.[3] By program operational characteristics we mean characteristics such as the following:

- program procedures,
- organizational arrangement,
- staffing pattern,
- management style (e.g., participatory, authoritarian),
- degree of staff communication,
- amount of staff training.

Such characteristics can have major impacts on program success.

---

3. The existence of variations and the importance of examining them to make evaluations more useful is becoming more widely recognized. See, for example, Reference 33, especially page 170.

These operational characteristics are each determined to some extent by program management. Thus, information on variations in operational characteristics and their relation to program outcomes can provide important clues on how to improve the program. An example:

> As part of the evaluation of the hot-meals-for-the-elderly program in Charlotte, North Carolina, the evaluators separated client ratings of food quality by whether the meals were prepared on-site or were catered. The ratings were significantly lower for meals at the facilities where the meals were catered. As a result, the program director sought space at all of the facilities for on-site meal preparation and began to work with the subcontractor on improving the quality of the catered meals.[4]

Ideally, all of the major variations in any program would be the subject of the evaluation, with attention focused from the start on all the variations and the data collected on each. In controlled experiments, clients would be assigned randomly to each variation.

In actual practice, however, evaluations seldom directly examine variations of more than a few program characteristics. Having formal comparison groups for more than a very few characteristics can impose an overwhelming burden on the evaluation, (especially controlled experiments) where adequate samples may not be available for many different combinations of characteristics.

A further complication is that evaluators are not likely at the beginning of an evaluation to be able to identify all of a program's critical characteristics. As the evaluators become familiar with the program's operation during the evaluation, they will likely find that other characteristics are having important effects. Thus, the plan for the evaluation should provide for an explicit search for major characteristics both initially during the evaluation. That search can use such procedures as interviews with program personnel and clients, and direct observation by the evaluators. Time should be made available to collect data on the characteristics identified and to analyze the data.

For example, during an evaluation of a team-policing experiment, a question could arise as to whether a significant part of the impact was due to the training given to team members. The evaluation team could then try to assess the amount of training provided to the members of each team, and as compared to the amount of training

---

4. Reference 59.

given other police officers. This could be done, even if only crudely, to ascertain whether there was some relation between outcomes and amount of training. If there was, the evaluators would report this as a possible explanatory factor. This, in turn, would indicate to police management whether more training was desirable and whether this should be in addition to, or perhaps in place of, team policing.

As with workload characteristics, outcome data can be examined against program characteristics to provide evidence, even though weak, as to whether program characteristics are related to outcomes. This requires the collecting of data on program characteristics and analysis of the data.

The extent to which generalizations can be made on the causal effects of such characteristics on outcomes will probably be quite limited. This will depend on the number of cases with each variation, the size of the differences in outcome among variations, and the presence of other plausible explanations for the observed relationships. For some evaluations (especially in local government), only a few cases may exist. For example, a city with only a few fire stations might undertake an evaluation to determine the effect of new pumpers at its stations. If the evaluators find that its stations provided significantly different amounts of training for the operators of the pumpers, an analysis should then be conducted relating the amount of training to differences in fire suppression effectiveness.

Examining a few cases, admittedly, is hardly sufficient to prove whether or not training is an important factor, but government managers are likely to find this added information useful and are likely to act on it. Given the alternative—that is, making decisions without the information—the use of even weak evidence seems appropriate.

The key issue is whether evaluations, especially those involving multiple projects or implementation at several locations, can provide information on the relationship of operational characteristics to outcomes. This step can require considerable additional resources; however, analyzing the outcomes of projects by their operational characteristics can greatly improve an evaluation's usefulness to managers. Program managers can then consider adopting operational characteristics associated with more successful projects or locations in their other projects or locations.

Except where it is practical to use random assignment to experimental and control groups, evaluations will be weak in their ability to identify which characteristics are causal. But even when cause-and-effect relationships are highly uncertain, any information on which program characteristics appear associated with success is likely to be helpful to program managers. At the very least, the information can suggest hypotheses as to which characteristics appear to make a difference, and these hypotheses can subsequently be examined in greater depth.

Obtaining Data on Reasons for Poor Outcomes along with the Outcome Information

In some evaluations, as part of the collection of basic evaluation data, information can also be obtained on the reasons for poor outcomes. For example, an evaluation of the effectiveness of police investigation should not be limited to determining the proportion of arrests that were dropped without prosecution. An effort should also be made to tabulate the number of arrests dropped for specific reasons, such as insufficient evidence or witness refusal to testify. Similarly, surveys of recreation program users should not only tally the proportion of citizens who did not use or did not like the program, but also should obtain information on their reasons for nonuse (e.g., the proportion of nonusers that reported the program was too far away, that they did not know about the program) and their reasons for dissatisfaction (e.g., the program's hours were inconvenient, program personnel did a poor job, equipment or facilities were poor). In neither of these examples would the added information on reasons for poor outcomes be costly to obtain.

Tallies of the reasons for poor outcomes should be useful both in interpreting the extent to which the outcomes were due to problems controllable by the agency and in providing clues as to what is wrong and how it might be corrected. If a substantial proportion of the respondents to a survey say that a recreation program's hours of operation are inconvenient, for example, the agency should consider altering the hours. Or if citizens in one neighborhood say they are too busy to use the program, this may indicate that the program is not needed in that neighborhood.

The following is an example of how a tally of the reasons for a poor outcome can provide suggestions for improvement:

> In the Phoenix evaluation of its emergency-only patrol car program, the evaluators collected information on why there were problems responding to emergency calls on the second shift. They found that in 83 percent of the cases the emergency-only car could not respond because it had a previous call; in the other 17 percent the car was out of service. This information indicated that the

problem was due to lack of cars and prompted the evaluators to recommend the addition of more emergency-only patrol cars to that shift.[5]

A caution: Analysts need to be careful in interpreting client reasons for dissatisfaction or nonuse. The reasons are sometimes difficult for clients to articulate accurately. Useful clues can be obtained, however, if the interview questions are developed carefully.

Seeking Qualitative Information on Program Problems during the Course of the Evaluation

Evaluators will have numerous opportunities during the evaluation to gain insight into how a program works and what its programs are. It would be wasteful not to make use of this knowledge to suggest ways to alleviate problems.

Information on program operations can come from interviews with program personnel and program clients as well as the evaluators' own observations. These same sources were suggested to help identify evaluation criteria and to identify program characteristics that should be examined for their relationship to outcomes. Thus, additional interviews solely for the purpose of obtaining information on program problems may not be necessary. Interviews undertaken either as an aid in formulating the evaluation design or obtaining data on program outcomes afford an excellent opportunity for obtaining information on a program's problems as well.

The following are two examples of how qualitative information can be instrumental in the evaluation of governmental programs:

> During an evaluation of San Diego County's food stamp program, the evaluators found that clients at welfare centers spent lengthy amounts of time waiting and that a high proportion of them were required to return to the centers with additional documentation. Having observed these inefficiencies, the evaluators made suggestions for improvement. These were subsequently implemented, and a second, post implementation, evaluation found significant improvements.[6]

> As part of the Phoenix evaluation of its emergency-only patrol car program, evaluators made on-site observations by riding in the patrol cars. The evaluators found no significant operating problems

5. Reference 75.

6. See References 78 and 83.

whose correction would have eliminated the need for the additional cars that the evaluators ultimately recommended.[7]

CAUTION: Program evaluations will seldom be able to provide definitive information as to what is wrong and how to correct it. The evaluation should, however, provide clues as to which problems warrant attention. Program evaluators should avoid becoming overly assertive in saying what program improvements are needed. The evidence is likely to be circumstantial and not conclusive, and actions that seem appropriate based on the evaluators' evidence may turn out to be infeasible or disregard other major considerations. It is much easier to suggest improvements than to implement them.

If these precautions are observed, efforts to help program officials improve the evaluated programs should greatly enhance the demand for program evaluation in state and local governments.

---

7. Reference 75.

VI. PUTTING IT ALL TOGETHER: INSTITUTIONAL ISSUES

Role of the Chief Executive

The following suggestions apply both to chief executive or administrative officers responsible for many operating agencies and to heads of individual agencies who want an internal evaluation capability.

The chief executive has ultimate responsibility for evaluation of his or her jurisdiction's programs. Although other responsibilities will probably prevent deep involvement, the chief executive's support for evaluation remains essential. The following are appropriate responsibilities for the chief executive:

1. Assign responsibility for program evaluations to units capable of conducting them objectively.
2. See that evaluations are relevant to the needs of decision makers by:

   - providing for a work schedule, and monitoring it, so that evaluation findings are available when needed for decision making;
   - providing for careful reviews of the objectives, effectiveness criteria, and clientele groups considered in the evaluation; and
   - taking a personal role, to the extent possible, in selecting the programs to be evaluated.

3. Support and encourage efforts to conduct objective and comprehensive evaluations by:

   - providing a level of staffing sufficient for each evaluation's schedule and scope, and preventing the diversion of evaluation staff to day-to-day operating problems; and
   - encouraging agency heads and other government personnel to cooperate with and assist evaluators.

4. Review and utilize the findings. Evaluations will be wasted effort if they are not taken seriously by those in authority.

Furthermore, without clear indications of interest and use on the part of the chief executive, future evaluations will not be taken seriously by other employees of the government.

5. Encourage agencies and program managers to provide for regular evaluations and to use the findings to improve their programs.

Part of these functions can be performed by the central administrative staff, with brief review by the chief executive officer. Beyond this, the executive can have an important effect on the quality and use of evaluations by providing a supportive "climate," making it clear that objective assessments of program effectiveness are valued.

Selection and Scheduling of Programs to Be Evaluated

Resources for program evaluation in local and state governments are and will continue to be scarce. Consequently, it is important to select programs for evaluations so that the most timely and useful information will be produced.

Jurisdictions of 100,000 population or more could initially assign one or two full-time central-staff members to program evaluation. More personnel and resources could be made available when the value of systematic program evaluation to local decision makers becomes more apparent. A reasonable target after this capability is developed might be one full-scale program evaluation per major agency each year—four to eight program evaluations each year "sponsored" and monitored by the central staff. Individual agencies might undertake additional evaluations as the need arises, and their resources allow.

Exhibit 15 lists several criteria for selecting subjects for evaluation. Some of these criteria may seem obvious, but in actual practice they are often neglected. In the design phase of individual evaluations a review should be made to assure that criteria such as those listed in Exhibit 15 are met to a reasonable degree. To assess whether the program is actually in place and sufficiently stable to warrant an evaluation of its impacts, the evaluators will need to take a careful look at the program. The importance of this is illustrated by the following example:

Michigan's Department of Social Services decided to conduct an evaluation of a new program of employment and training for welfare clients. An experimental design was selected, and a county that was thought to have a well-developed program was chosen to be the focus of the study. After the study began, however, it was found that the county's program was still in the development stage. Rather than drop the evaluation, the state evaluation team provided assistance to the county in setting up the program, and the evaluation period was extended. The evaluators noted two possible adverse consequences from the situation: (1) since the program was in the development state for its first three months, the results might be not generally applicable; (2) as a result of the state's help, the county workers became very aware of the study, and this awareness may have affected their performance.[1]

This process of careful review of a program before a full evaluation begins, along with corrective action to make a program more evaluable, has become known as "evaluability assessment."[2]

Programs to be evaluated should be selected after consultation with the chief executive, department heads, program managers, and central staffs (such as budget, research, or planning offices). Legislative requirements, and the interests of legislators, can also have a major bearing on which programs are chosen for evaluation.

It may be wise, however, to concentrate initial evaluation efforts on new programs or on existing programs being considered for expansion, since evaluation of existing programs may antagonize the programs' large or politically powerful constituencies.

To reduce the risk that funds will be wasted, two strategies seem particularly useful:

- Wherever possible, make continued funding of new programs or significant expansion of existing programs contingent on positive findings from an in-depth evaluation (after an appropriate period of operation).
- Introduce a new program on a pilot scale rather than beginning it on a full scale, if possible. An evaluation would then be conducted before deciding on further implementation. (This alternative may not be practical when a program involves a large, one-time start-up cost, such as for new facilities.)

It is highly desirable that a state or local government prepare an annual evaluation plan. The evaluation plans of each agency should be included in the plan, and each evaluation should be given an

---

1. See Reference 65.

2. See References 40 and 51. Reference 33 also encourages the use of these steps but does not use the term "evaluability assessment."

Exhibit 15.   CRITERIA FOR SELECTING ISSUES FOR
PROGRAM EVALUATION

Can the results of the evaluation influence decisions about the program?

—Programs for which a decision regarding continuation, modification, or termination needs to be made are obvious candidates.

—Poor candidates are those about which decision makers have strong preconceptions of program value or for which there is considerable support by influential interest groups if these circumstances make it very unlikely that the program would be altered. In some cases, however, the program may be of such great importance to a community that government officials may proceed with the evaluation and be prepared to seek changes despite political risks.

—Can the evaluation be completed in time to be helpful to decision makers? Evaluations completed after public officials become committed to a decision are useless.

Can the evaluation be done?

—Are sufficient data obtainable on important effects of the program? Program evaluations can never cover all effects, but before an evaluation is begun it should be clear that it will be possible to gather meaningful data on significant aspects of the program. For example, the long-term impacts of job training, health, or education programs may not appear for many years. In most cases, governments are unable to wait this long. Nevertheless, *intermediate* results can often be made available and thus provide significant information for interim decisions.

—Can sufficient resources be obtained to meet the time schedule and technical requirements of the evaluation?

—Is the program actually in place, and is it being implemented as originally planned? If not, an evaluation may not be appropriate.

—Has the program been stable enough so that an evaluation will provide relevant information? A program that is constantly changing or is about to change in significant ways is not a good candidate for evaluation.

Exhibit 15 (continued)

Is the program significant enough to merit evaluation?

—Programs that involve a large amount of government resources or that have important potential benefits or possible negative consequences to the public should be given higher priority. Thus, the likely cost of the evaluation should be compared to the possible decreased cost or improved effectiveness that may result.

—Is the program suspected of being marginal in its performance? If so, there may be opportunities for making major improvements or cost reductions. Relatively old programs that have not received an in-depth evaluation in a long time may fit this criterion.

—Is the program a new one whose potential benefits and costs are particularly uncertain? The program should be reviewed after operating long enough to demonstrate its effectiveness. This probably means a minimum of six months to one year of operation for most programs, though even these time periods are often too short for evaluating long-term effects. New programs are often more open to alteration because they have not yet gained a strong constituency.

—Programs that are candidates for expansion are particularly suitable candidates for an evaluation.

---

explicit schedule with a completion date. The schedules should be determined with the participation of central and agency staffs, but, as noted earlier, agency managers should be allowed to schedule additional evaluations if funds are available and the managers believe that additional evaluations will be useful. The schedules should be monitored by the central staff to assure that the evaluations are completed in time to be useful for decision making. The central staff might also be given authority to review and approve agency evaluation plans to assure that government-wide concerns are included.

Evaluation needs should be considered before major new programs are implemented. This will increase the likelihood that the necessary baseline data will be collected both before and while the new program is under way. This can considerably strengthen the evaluation. Most evaluations are done after a program has been operating for a time, making it difficult to acquire adequate preprogram data. This thwarts the comparison of before and after program data that is the heart of most evaluations.

Who Should Be Responsible for Evaluation?

Administrators face a dilemma when they have to decide whether to assign responsibility for conducting an evaluation to the central or operating level staff.

It is essential not only that the evaluation be conducted objectively but also that potential users of the evaluation believe that it was conducted impartially. Therefore, in general, *staffs that operate the program should not be responsible for its formal evaluation.* Otherwise, the credibility of the evaluation may be compromised.

On the other hand, several factors make the cooperation and active participation of program staff in an evaluation highly desirable:

- Much of the information about a program is lodged with those immediately responsible for the program.
- Program modifications suggested by the evaluation will have to be implemented by program personnel. These modifications are likely to be implemented more effectively if program personnel understand and accept the evaluation's conclusions and the process used to reach them.
- Agency and program heads should be encouraged to recognize that part of their management responsibility is to evaluate their programs periodically and objectively.

The following set of arrangements is probably workable:

1. *Whenever possible, a central staff unit should have overall responsibility for evaluation within the government.* A separate program evaluation staff is probably most feasible in very large jurisdictions. Nevertheless, states and local jurisdictions with populations of more than 100,000 would appear to be capable of supporting at least a small central staff for program analysis and evaluation. When these functions are carried out by the same staff unit, it is more likely that evaluations of past performance will be fully utilized in analyzing future program alternatives. To increase the probability that the findings will be used, such a unit might be part of the state, city, or county budget office. If located in the budget office, however, there is a danger that the evaluation staff will frequently be diverted to "firefighting" duties.

In a jurisdiction with a population of about 100,000, it would be reasonable to think that a one- to two-person evaluation staff could monitor four to six program evaluations per year.

As an alternative approach, the central staff might delegate much of the actual evaluation effort to individual operating agencies, or where an evaluation involved more than a single agency, to an ad hoc interagency task force. In these cases the central staff should monitor the evaluations to insure that their scope, methodology, and basic assumptions (including objectives and criteria) are adequate.

2. *Operating agency heads should be encouraged to sponsor systematic evaluations of programs within their areas of responsibility.* In most cases they should assign responsibility for conducting the evaluation to a unit at a higher organizational level than the program being evaluated.

Large agencies, especially those with multimillion dollar budgets, should have full-time program analysis and evaluation staffs. Evaluations of specific police programs, for example, would ordinarily be undertaken by the planning, evaluation, and research unit of the police department. However, for police programs of major community concern or that significantly involved other agencies (such as the corrections and court systems), evaluation would be better directed by a higher level unit, such as an interagency team or the central staff.

With single-agency evaluations there is a danger that the problem will be defined too narrowly, with objectives and evaluation criteria being limited to the duties of the particular agency. Police agencies, for example, might ignore the disposition of arrests; transportation agencies might neglect air and noise pollution. Review and assistance by a central evaluation staff would reduce this possibility.

3. *Managers of programs being evaluated should participate in the evaluation.* Program managers should help identify program objectives, evaluation criteria, clientele groups, specific data requirements and problems, and even the evaluation design. Their knowledge of the program is too valuable not to be utilized. Ignoring them in designing the evaluation is hazardous and may result in the omission of important program considerations.

Another approach is to have operating staff work closely with central evaluation staff during the course of the evaluation. This has the advantages of bringing program knowledge to the evaluation, training additional staff in evaluation techniques, and involving program staff who can then be assigned the responsibility for implementing the changes recommended as a result of the evaluation.

It is also advisable to ask program personnel to review the data used in the evaluation and the first draft of the evaluation before the evaluation is completed. This reduces the likelihood of misinterpretation of the data by outside evaluators. (To avoid subsequent disclaimers, it may be advisable to obtain a written statement from the agency as to the appropriateness of the evaluation data.)

4. *Program evaluation should preferably be combined with program analysis, the examination of future courses of action.* Program evaluation should be intended to help determine future actions. It is therefore preferable, and most useful, to have an evaluation unit that not only examines information on past performance but also uses that information to assess alternative future actions. Very similar skills are involved in both tasks. This applies whether the evaluation unit is in a central staff office or in an operating department.[3]

Type of Staff and Training Needed

Most of the steps in a program evaluation do not require highly specialized professional training, but they do require a systematic, analytical approach. Some state and local governments already have some staff members capable of undertaking many parts of an evaluation. With adequate training and guidance, such a capability is within reach of many others. The principal steps are the following:

- The first priority is to obtain someone with considerable expertise to supervise the technical aspects of evaluation. This person would also be responsible for providing on-the-job training to others. Unfortunately, existing salary scales often prevent state and local governments from attracting professional evaluators as employees.
- Most local governments and state agencies will try to rely on existing staff. This means concentrating on limited-scope evaluations and, at the same time, using on-the-job training opportunities and training materials to increase the technical skill of the present staff. The technical requirements for annual outcome monitoring are less demanding than those for individual program evaluations. Developing monitoring procedures can help develop the internal capability for in-depth program evaluation and may be a practical first step.
- Existing capabilities can be supplemented by the use of consultants. Some of the program evaluation and data collection techniques described in Chapters 3 and 4 require specially trained personnel whom few local governments are likely to employ on a full-time basis (such as statistical technicians to estimate the

---

3. A discussion of "program analysis" is contained in "Program Analysis for State and Local Governments," The Urban Institute, Washington, D.C., 1976.

statistical significance of observed changes in evaluation criteria or to design sampling plans). Outside assistance may also be useful for specific technical aspects of an evaluation, for training assistance, or for undertaking highly complex or controversial evaluations. The use of consultants is discussed further in the next section.

Training opportunities in program evaluation for state and local government staffs are limited, but an increasing number of universities are providing courses in evaluation. In addition, the literature on program evaluation is large and of generally good quality. And there is an increasing amount of good case study material.[4]

Many governments that want to upgrade their analytical capabilities have found it difficult to find persons with both quantitative skills and a broad understanding of governmental processes. However, this problem appears to be easing somewhat as graduate schools of public administration and various specific professional fields expose students to an increasing amount of quantitative material. The technical fields of engineering, operations research, and economics are beginning to introduce more applicable subject matter and are producing a greater number of students interested in state and local government employment.

The Use of Outside Consultants

Outside consultants can be used to perform the following tasks:

- Supplement an internal evaluation team—perhaps specialized skills not available internally. Outside consultants, for example, might be retained to undertake citizen surveys for either annual outcome monitoring or for specific program evaluations.
- Provide training to in-house evaluation personnel.
- Perform complete evaluations. The advantages and disadvantages of using outside consultants are summarized in Exhibit 16.

State and local governments can draw upon a variety of sources of outside assistance, including private firms and universities. In addition, the staffs of councils of governments and other regional planning bodies may be available for short-term assistance.

---

4. See, for example, the items listed in the second section of the References.

Exhibit 16.   ADVANTAGES AND DISADVANTAGES OF
RETAINING OUTSIDE CONSULTANTS TO
PERFORM AN ENTIRE PROGRAM
EVALUATION

Advantages

Since consultants are not permanent members of the government organization, they are less likely to have a stake in the outcome than are
members of either the central or operating level staffs. Therefore, they
are more likely to be able to provide needed objectivity.

When a program is particularly controversial, evaluations conducted
by outside consultants may provide needed credibility outside the government.

Outside consultants may have specialized skills that are necessary
because the program being evaluated is complex or highly technical.
Some outside consultants may also have a broader view of the program
because they are familiar with similar programs in other jurisdictions.

Evaluation personnel may not be available internally to complete the
evaluation within the required time.

Disadvantages

Costs and time requirements are likely to be greater than if the evaluation were done internally. This is partly because an outside group must
become familiar with the situation in the jurisdiction before undertaking
the evaluation.

An outside group may not have a sufficient perspective of the government's needs in defining problems and presenting findings.

Outside consultants may be regarded as more of a threat than an internal group and therefore may meet more resistance in gathering data and
eliciting the participation of program personnel. In some situations,
however, it may be easier for an outside consultant to obtain internal
cooperation.

Because outside consultants do not have a continuing relationship
with policy officials, their findings may be less likely to be used in subsequent program decisions.

When using consultants to perform an evaluation, the following
controls should be instituted by the local or state government to
insure that the final product is relevant to the needs of decision
makers:

- The government should review the statement of program objectives, the evaluation criteria, the clientele groups to be consid-

ered, and the general scope and methodology to be used in the study before any data are collected.

- There should be clear agreement on a schedule. Findings that come too late for decision making may make the evaluation a wasted effort.
- There should be a specific agreement on the amount and type of staff assistance which the government will provide, as well as an agreement on the data to which the evaluators will have access.
- The government should assure that the consultant has adequate access to the various government agencies from which data are to be obtained.
- Governmental staff should periodically check both the consultant's progress and procedures. Periodic progress reports (e.g., monthly) to government officials should be required.
- The consultant's final report should be in writing, and the consultant should also provide an oral briefing. The consultant should document major assumptions and procedures. All data used should be provided to the government in understandable form (but conforming to confidentiality requirements).

Presentation of Results

Inadequate presentation of findings has ruined many good analyses. Government officials should insist on clear and thorough presentation of an evaluation's results. The following suggestions may make the evaluation report more usable by decision makers:

- *Program evaluation findings should be in writing.* This reduces the possibility that misunderstandings will develop over evaluation findings or their interpretation. Errors or poor methodology may not be apparent and cannot be checked unless the findings are in written form. Even though government policy officials may not have the time to read such material, a staff member who did not participate in the study should review it carefully to assure that the study's scope, procedures, and findings appear reasonable. Written reports should generally be supplemented by oral presentations to decision makers.
- *Agencies involved in the evaluation should have an opportunity to review the evaluation report before it is put in final form.* Their reactions and suggestions will often add to the overall perspective, and occasionally they will detect major omissions in the evaluation report that can either be corrected

or considered in future decisions. It is expected that agency or program personnel may disagree with the findings, especially when the evaluation produces negative ones. A government may want to provide space in the final report for program offices to respond to the findings of the evaluation team.

- *The form of presentation should be tailored to the preferences of key officials.* Some prefer tables, others prefer charts and graphs. Others may want only oral summaries.

Utilization and Follow-Up of Evaluation Results

Seldom will a program evaluation, by itself, tell government administrators what should be done in the future. Thus, a major use of program evaluation data is to provide information from which estimates can be made of the costs and impacts likely to occur if the same program, or some variation of it, is continued.

> For example, the evaluation of the Indianapolis Take-Home Car Plan provided information on its cost and effectiveness. But whether more or fewer funds should be applied to such a plan should not be decided until local officials have considered the potential costs and benefits of other ways to spend the funds (such as for additional foot patrols or street lighting).

A program evaluation, in short, should be followed by the development and analysis of alternatives. This is a crucial step which may determine the usefulness of the entire effort.

A second need is to provide for follow-up on decisions made as a result of evaluation findings. A first step is to arrange for postmortems of the evaluation with agency and program officials soon after an evaluation has been completed. If done in a constructive way, these postmortems can encourage agency and program personnel to make modifications whose need is indicated by the evaluation.

A decision to modify a program should lead to an explicit modification schedule and monitoring of the schedule to assure proper implementation. This action is often neglected and often results in action being delayed or deferred indefinitely.

The Cost of Program Evaluation

The cost of program evaluations can vary considerably. Many evaluations of major federal programs cost hundreds of thousands of dollars. Program evaluations by state and local governments will normally entail several months of evaluators' time. The evaluation of the Indianapolis Take-Home Car Plan required approximately three staff-months of effort.[5] More thorough and complex evaluations may require from six staff-months to several staff-years of effort. The evaluation of Nashville's programs of short-term care for neglected-dependent children and the evaluation of Dade County's drug abuse treatment program each required about one to two staff-years of professional time plus computer assistance.[6] These figures do not include the effort of various program personnel who assisted the evaluators from time to time.

A reasonable way to consider evaluation costs is to relate them to the magnitude of the program being evaluated. A figure of 0.5 to 2 percent of program funds for program evaluation has been applied to federal programs, programs that usually involve millions of dollars.[7] A figure of 1 to 2 percent for a four-year program with annual costs of $500,000 would mean spending between $20,000 and $40,000 for evaluation over the life of the program.

Possible Funding Sources for Program Evaluations

In most cases, state and local governments will have to rely on their own funds for program evaluation. However, the federal government sometimes provides funds that can be used for evaluation by state and local agencies. Often federal agencies are amenable to evaluation components in proposals for new programs. State and local governments could regularly incorporate a program evaluation component in their proposals.

The Limitations of Program Evaluation

The limitations of program evaluation should be recognized.

- Inherent technical problems may prevent identification of direct causal relationships between program activities and specific outcomes. This is the major concern of the evaluation designs described in Chapter 3.
- Some program impacts are difficult to identify or measure quantitatively. Chapter 2, and some of the data collection techniques described in Chapter 4, address this problem.

---

5. Reference 62.

6. References 56 and 57.

7. See Reference 52.

- The numbers provided by an evaluation are not scientific truths. Many human judgments are involved in the selection of criteria, the evaluation design, the type of data collected, and the presentation of findings. The data themselves are also subject to limitations and inaccuracies.
- Program evaluation cannot, by itself, indicate whether a program was or is worth its cost. Inevitably, any program will affect different objectives and different population segments in different ways. Various weighting systems for combining measurements of the various criteria can be designed, but public officials must make the final judgments themselves.[8] In addition, the question always remains whether using the resources for some other purpose (no matter how well, or how poorly, the program has performed) would be more beneficial.

Not all program evaluations will be useful. Some will have to be aborted because conditions change during the study. Others will fail to produce an adequate basis for decisions regarding the program. In addition, it is probably true that many evaluations (including those for the federal government) have been a waste of money because of poor design, poor planning, poor implementation, unavailability of data, inadequate funding, or a combination of these.

Despite these limitations, however, systematic evaluations, reasonably and thoughtfully done, should provide a better basis for decisions about the programs evaluated. Evaluation is a management tool. It must, in the end, demonstrate its worth by leading to reduced costs or improved effectiveness of government programs.

---

8. Imparting monetary values to each evaluation criterion for calculating a single net "dollar value" or cost-benefit ratio is occasionally proposed. Imputations like these, however, are seldom adequate to represent the various nonmonetary criteria.

Appendix A. A CASE STUDY OF EVALUATION IN ACTION: OPERATION CLEAN SWEEP

In August, September, and October, 1971, the District of Columbia conducted Operation Clean Sweep, an intensive, one-time effort to remove accumulated litter and other solid wastes.[1] It was a heavily publicized campaign utilizing several hundred regular and supplemental cleaning personnel over a two-month period who concentrated each week on one of the nine neighborhood service areas in the District of Columbia. The workers cleaned streets and alleys and collected refuse set out by residents. Residents were encouraged to clean private property—homes, backyards, vacant lots—and to set out refuse for collection. The goal of this combination of government and citizen effort was to achieve both an immediate and a lasting improvement in neighborhood cleanliness.

The District's Department of Environmental Services was responsible for solid waste collection, and the department's Division of Solid Waste Collection had immediate responsibility for performing Operation Clean Sweep.

The department's Division of Program Planning and Review conducted an evaluation of Operation Clean Sweep with the assistance of The Urban Institute. The division staff was selected because it was part of the department with operating responsibility, and any recommendations that it might make for improvements in the operation were more likely to be implemented. Since the division reported directly to the department's administrator, it seemed likely that it could objectively evaluate Operation Clean Sweep. Both the mayor's staff and the head of the solid waste collection operation reviewed key points of the study with the evaluators.

Operation Clean Sweep aimed at improving neighborhood cleanliness and, as a result, the health, safety, and appearance of the District by reducing the amount of uncollected solid waste at as low a cost as possible. The mayor's staff and the department also wanted

---

1. More information on this evaluation and on procedures for measuring the effectiveness of solid waste collection can be found in Reference 5.

to know if such an intensive program would have any lasting effect on the city's general cleanliness.

The program was evaluated on the basis of the following criteria:

- Changes in street and alley cleanliness ratings. Two measures were used: average visual ratings for an area and the percentage of streets and alleys with ratings worse than a targeted cleanliness level.
- Changes in citizen perceptions of solid waste collection services, including cleanliness, odors, noise, and missed collections.
- Program costs.

The clientele groups affected were primarily the residents in each of the nine neighborhood service areas. Therefore, data on the evaluation criteria (other than cost) were collected for each of the nine service areas as well as for the city as a whole.

Ideally, it would have been desirable to measure the direct effects (such as illness or injury) of uncollected solid waste on the city's health and safety, but such data were not available in usable form. Instead, it was assumed that these effects were directly related to street cleanliness. Thus, the criteria used in the evaluation were assumed to be adequate proxies for health and safety.

A potentially negative effect of the operation was delay of refuse collections in service areas not being concentrated on that week. Though normal twice-a-week collection was maintained in all service areas, the need for major cleaning forces in the service area being intensely cleaned might cause some delays and reduce special pickups in other neighborhoods. Program cost, of course, was the other important criterion.

Evaluation Procedure

Design Number 1 in Chapter 3, before vs. after comparison, was the design used to evaluate Operation Clean Sweep. Although this design is the least sophisticated of the designs presented in Chapter 3, the data collection procedures used for it were quite advanced for local government. In this instance, use of the design seemed appropriate. Time trend projection (Design Number 2) was not possible because the District of Columbia had only recently begun rating street and alley cleanliness conditions and had conducted no relevant citizen surveys. Consequently, no prior-year data were available. Comparison with other jurisdictions (Design Number 3) was not possible because data on the criteria were not available from other local jurisdictions. Few jurisdictions, if any, systematically measure street cleanliness or citizen satisfaction with the cleanliness of their neighborhoods.

Because the evaluation was planned in advance of the program, it was possible to collect preprogram data. To test the program's effectiveness fully, it might have been desirable to provide different variations of the operation in different service areas. As often is likely to be the case, just getting approval for an evaluation was a major accomplishment; an attempt to complicate the program's operation by introducing planned variations would have been a major undertaking. The campaign had been announced as a city-wide effort before the evaluation was planned; consequently, evaluation by controlled experimentation (Design Number 4) was not feasible either.

Because the city did not set specific targets for the program, no targets were available for comparison with actual achievements (Design Number 5). One reason why targets were not set was that officials had little experience with the collecting of the special data used in the evaluation.

Two special data collection procedures were used. Both had earlier been developed and tested in the District of Columbia to provide annual outcome monitoring of solid waste collection. These were visual cleanliness ratings and a citizen survey:

Visual Ratings of Cleanliness by Inspectors

A series of photographs were selected for a cleanliness rating scale. Each photograph represented a grade of street or alley cleanliness—from Condition 1, the cleanest, to Condition 4, the most littered. Exhibit 17 shows four of the photos used for the alley rating scale.

A sample of streets and alleys in each of the nine service areas was then selected.[2] A week before the special cleanup was conducted in a service area, one of the three inspectors assigned to the program rated the cleanliness of the streets and alleys in the sample, using the photographic rating scale. (The inspector drove down the streets and recorded his ratings on tape, which were subsequently transcribed.) The inspector returned a week after the cleanup and rated

---

2. The sample was quite large, with 100 percent coverage in areas believed to be heavily littered. Data on specific streets were also used for operational purposes, such as identifying streets needing special attention.

Exhibit 17.   EXAMPLES OF ALLEY LITTER CONDITIONS

Condition 1. Clean

Condition 2. Moderately Clean

Exhibit 17. (continued)

Condition 3. Moderately Littered

Condition 4. Heavily Littered

the cleanliness of the streets and alleys in the sample a second time. To test the durability of the improvement, streets in the sample were also rated two months later.

Citizen Survey

To obtain information on citizen satisfaction, interviews were conducted with approximately 100 randomly selected householders in an area composed of two neighborhood service areas. They were questioned about their perceptions of neighborhood cleanliness, odors from uncollected solid waste, noise during collections, and missed collections.

Time did not permit a telephone survey of households immediately before Operation Clean Sweep started. However, as part of a test of procedures for an outcome monitoring system, 101 households in two of the nine neighborhood service areas had been surveyed by telephone about street cleanliness in April, four months before Operation Clean Sweep.

Telephone interviews were again conducted in these two service areas approximately four months after the special cleanup. Half of the interviews were with households in the first sample and half were with new households. The questionnaire used for the second set of interviews included four questions directly relating to Operation Clean Sweep (e.g., "Have you noticed any change in the cleanliness of your neighborhood in the last 3 to 4 months?"). Otherwise, the questions asked in the first and second surveys were, with a few minor changes, the same.

Interviews with a sample of the households in the other seven service areas were also planned but were prevented by personnel vacations in the department.

Evaluation Results

Summary data from the visual ratings of cleanliness are displayed in Exhibit 18. The exhibit shows the average rating and the percentage of ratings 2.5 or higher for each of the nine service areas and for the whole city. In addition to the data shown in the exhibit, tables and maps were prepared that identified census tracts and groups of blocks with particularly bad conditions.

Some of the results of the telephone surveys are illustrated in Exhibit 19.

As indicated by the decline in the percentage of streets rated 2.5 or higher (Exhibit 18), conditions in some of the more littered areas did

Exhibit 18. PROGRAM EVALUATION FINDINGS: STREET
CLEANLINESS RATINGS BEFORE AND AFTER
OPERATION CLEAN SWEEP

Service Area	Average Rating			Percent of Streets with Ratings of 2.5 or Higher		
	Before	After	Change	Before	After	Change
1	1.5	1.5	0	3	1	- 2
2	1.7	1.6	-0.1	19	5	-14
3	1.8	1.7	-0.1	21	12	- 9
4	1.9	1.4	-0.5	20	7	-13
5	1.8	1.8	0	21	15	- 6
6	2.2	2.3	+0.1	46	47	+ 1
7	2.1	1.5	-0.6	40	6	-34
8	1.4	1.4	0	0	0	0
9	1.4	1.6	+0.2	4	4	0
D.C. Total	1.8	1.7	-0.1	19	11	-8

Note: 1. Ratings were on a scale of 1.0 to 4.0. The higher the number, the worse
the conditions.
2. A third inspection conducted in selected service areas two to three
months following the second inspection revealed that, generally, conditions had regressed to a point midway between the conditions before
and after cleanups.

improve. To some extent, however, this improvement was achieved
at the cost of a slight worsening of conditions on cleaner streets.
Thus, the average cleanliness of neighborhoods did not change
markedly.

In the two service areas surveyed by telephone (Exhibit 19), citizens' perceptions of the cleanliness of the streets on which they
lived (Question 1) became more favorable. However, the difference
was not sufficiently large to describe the change as statistically significant. A substantial percentage perceived some improvement
during the period of Clean Sweep (Question 2)—38 percent said
their streets were cleaner, only 5 percent said they were dirtier.

Consequently, there appeared to be a greater perception of improvement in these two areas (Areas 3 and 4) than that indicated by

Exhibit 19. PROGRAM EVALUATION FINDINGS: RESPONSES TO CITIZEN SURVEY[a]

	PERCENTAGE RESPONSES	
	April 1971 4 months *Before* Clean Sweep	*December 1971* 4 months *After* Clean Sweep
QUESTION:	(101 Respondents)	(110 Respondents)
(1) What do you think of the cleanliness of the street you live on?		
a. Clean	14	13
b. Mostly clean	45	50
c. Fairly dirty	27	24
d. Very dirty	14	13
e. No opinion	0	0
% Satisfied (a + b)	59 ± 8	63 ± 7
% Dissatisfied (c + d)	41 ∓ 8	37 ∓ 7
(2) Have you noticed any change in the cleanliness of your streets in the last 3 or 4 months? (Not asked in the April survey.)		
a. Very much cleaner		10
b. Somewhat cleaner		28
c. Somewhat dirtier	not	3
d. Very much dirtier	applicable	2
e. No change noticed		52
f. Don't know/no opinion		5
(3) How often do the collectors spill trash and garbage or leave some that you have set out?		
a. Hardly ever	64	56
b. Once a month	8	16
c. More than once a month	23	26
d. Don't know/no opinion	5	2
% Satisfied (a)	67 ± 9	57 ± 8
% Dissatisfied (b + c)	33 ∓ 9	43 ∓ 8

Note: The ranges shown indicate the approximate statistical confidence limits (90 percent).
a. Service areas 3 and 4 combined.

the inspection ratings (Exhibit 18). This may have occurred because dirty areas have a disproportionate effect on perceptions of cleanliness. The percentage of dirty streets, however, was significantly reduced in both of these two areas (Exhibit 18).

The evaluators did not observe any other factors that could have accounted for the changes in cleanliness that occurred. Weather conditions were stable, and no other major changes were made in other city programs during the time period covered by the evaluation. The evaluation's major weakness was that it did not control for other factors, leaving some doubt as to whether the changes could be attributed solely to the program being evaluated. However, the program's relatively short time span made it less likely that external factors played any significant part in the change.

It also was not possible with this design to separate the effects of the actual physical cleanup procedures from the effects of the publicity given the program. (Sixty-seven percent of the citizens surveyed said they knew what Operation Clean Sweep was.)

The program's long-term effects, as noted in the footnote of Exhibit 18, were apparently not great. However, additional observations and surveys, perhaps in another six months, would have been needed to evaluate long-term effects more accurately.

The Department of Environmental Services estimated the total direct cost of Operation Clean Sweep at $446,000. This figure included approximately $416,000 for overtime and $30,000 for materials, such as gloves, signs, brooms, shovels, bags, printing, and publicity. These costs did not include maintenance and depreciation of department equipment, costs which would have been incurred in any case.

Cost of the Evaluation

Because the basic procedures for both the inspection rating system and the telephone survey had been established before the evaluation of Operation Clean Sweep, the cost of identifying objectives, criteria, and methods of data collection was minimal. The total cost of the evaluation was approximately $47,000. Most of the work, however, was done by permanent employees, and the out-of-pocket cost was actually less than $6,000.

The visual rating of street cleanliness was the most costly aspect of the evaluation, primarily because a large sample of city blocks was examined and maps of inspection routes had to be laid out. The three inspectors worked nearly full time during the four-month period of pre- and postprogram inspections. An additional two to three person-years of effort by analytical and clerical personnel were required.

The telephone survey required about 25 person-hours for the 110 interviews. A full set of interviews of 1,200 persons (600 households covering all service areas before and 600 after Clean Sweep) would have required about two person-months to complete.

How It Was Used

Reports summarizing the visual inspection and interview data were submitted to the director of the Department of Environmental Services and then presented orally.

The evaluation of Operation Clean Sweep was subsequently used in four ways:

- To identify the effectiveness of the campaign in reducing particular problems. The city was disappointed by the lack of major improvements in street cleanliness and decided because of the costs involved not to continue the program on a regular basis.
- To guide department personnel in their attempts to design programs aimed at specific problems (such as particularly dirty alleys).
- To identify the desirability of future requests for similar efforts to reduce neighborhood solid waste.
- Data on the cleanliness of specific blocks were also used for operational purposes to guide the assignment of crews to trouble spots.

Appendix B. CONDITIONS UNDER WHICH CONTROLLED, RANDOMIZED EXPERIMENTS ARE LIKELY TO BE APPROPRIATE FOR STATE AND LOCAL GOVERNMENTS[1]

There are two principal requirements for controlled, randomized experiments (Evaluation Design 4 of Chapter 3):

1. Random assignment of units either to the experimental group served by the new program or to the one or more control groups not served by the new program. Random assignment means that each unit has the same chance of being assigned to any group.[2] Some procedure—such as flipping a coin or using a table of random numbers—is used to make each assignment. The units most commonly used are people, as in experiments involving treatment programs for clients (such as health, correctional, employment, or social service programs). The units can be other things, however, such as public facilities or geographical areas that receive different types or levels of service. In some experiments, random assignments are made only at the beginning; in other experiments, new units are randomly assigned to groups throughout the experimental period.

2. Sufficient control of conditions throughout the experimental period so that groups continue to receive the type and level of service intended, and so that random assignment continues (if necessary). For example, the Phoenix, Arizona, Alcohol Safety Action Program experiment (see Chapter 3) randomly assigned clients for nine months. Ideally, this means that neither group receives any special attention other than the planned intervention, thus avoiding the introduction of other factors that might affect the outcomes.

---

1. This section is adapted from Chapter 6 of Reference 11. Useful discussions of this subject are contained in References 7, 13, 36, and 37.

2. It is not necessary to restrict the number of groups to two. If more than one alternative treatment is to be tested, more than two groups should be used. The principle that each unit should have the same chance of being assigned to a group as every other unit still applies.

The evaluation procedures should be planned well ahead of the introduction of the new program, appropriate methods should be worked out to make and enforce random assignments, and the prescribed procedures should be followed throughout the experiment. (This is all much easier said than done.)

The use of controlled, randomized experiments has largely been absent from state and local government evaluation. But controlled, randomized experiments can strengthen considerably the conclusions of an evaluation. Such experiments are usually associated with expensive and comprehensive program evaluations. But sometimes they add little expense. And in other instances, it may be cheaper in the long run (especially if the social costs are considered) to do one conclusive evaluation using an experimental design than to do inconclusive studies using weaker designs.[3]

The following sections discuss the conditions under which controlled experiments are likely to be most appropriate for evaluating government programs. Exhibit 13 in Chapter 3 lists the conditions. (Many of these conditions also apply to the other evaluation designs, but they are of particular concern to experimental designs.)

1. *There is likely to be a high degree of ambiguity as to whether outcomes were caused by the program if some other evaluation design is used.* A less demanding design may be adequate, however, when the evaluation criteria are closely linked to the intervention. Many types of water pollution abatement and street cleanup programs, for example, are less likely to require controlled experiments because the observed physical changes in water quality or street cleanliness are more likely to be attributable to the interventions. Controlled experiments are particularly appropriate for evaluating human services programs. Controlled experiments are also less necessary for evaluating programs whose principal effects are expected to appear quickly (e.g., within a year) where there is less likelihood of external factors affecting the outcomes.

2. *Some citizens can be given different services than others without significant danger or harm.* If there is a substantial chance that withholding the program from the control group would cause them substantial harm, put them in substantial danger, or raise legal objections of discrimination, the experimental approach is not likely to be appropriate. (Very few state or local government programs, however, are likely to be of this type.)

---

3. Reference 61, p. 5.

The reverse also applies: if there is a possibility that the program may be dangerous to the experimental group, the usefulness of a controlled experiment becomes questionable. At the least, those who participate in the experimental group should be volunteers and should be fully aware of the potential ramifications of their participation. (This should be the case, of course, for any evaluation.)

An example is withdrawal or reduction of police or fire protection services in certain areas in order to test the effects of a new program. Here, the issue is the extent to which the withdrawal of service entails a major risk. In one experiment, for example, a police department varied the amount of patrol in randomly selected parts of the city.[4] In some areas, routine patrol was completely withdrawn and police responded only to service calls. The experiment was undertaken without major opposition and found no significant difference in the amount of crime in the different experimental areas.[5]

If public officials and the evaluators are in substantial agreement that withdrawal of a service is not likely to have harmful effects, and if the public itself does not disagree, an experiment with random assignment of units becomes feasible. If some public officials or part of the public believes otherwise, the experiment will be less feasible.

If the government believes that perceptions of the potential risks are exaggerated, it may try to change those perceptions. Since the ultimate purpose of experimentation is to improve government services or reduce government costs—both of which are attractive objectives to citizens—such efforts to change perceptions may succeed. The issue is whether the better evidence that can be obtained through controlled, randomized experiments is likely to contribute to the long-term health and safety of the community.

3. *Some citizens can be given different services than others without violating moral and ethical standards.* Some experiments, although not involving physical dangers, may call for not providing, or significantly reducing, a service to some groups. Ethical-moral issues may then be raised. For example, an experiment to assess the effectiveness of social casework might be designed in such a way as to prevent some clients from receiving services. This could be seen by some people as unethical or immoral.

---

4. Reference 64.

5. The study findings aroused controversy, but not on the grounds that the experiment was unsafe.

One way to reduce this kind of objection, and one which will be appropriate in many cases, is not to withdraw services fully from any client but to provide less drastic variations in services.

4. *There is substantial doubt about the effectiveness of a program.* The purpose of experimentation is to obtain information where there is considerable uncertainty about the effectiveness of the program that is the subject of the experiment. It has been argued that conducting programs with no evidence of their effectiveness, or with highly questionable evidence (such as that obtained from unrandomized evaluation designs), is itself unethical.[6]

5. *There are insufficient resources to provide the program to all clients.* Even when a program is generally accepted as being helpful, the resources necessary to provide it to all eligible clients may not be available. Rules (implicit or explicit) are then used to determine which clients will receive the service—usually first come, first served or priority to those most in need. If it is decided to evaluate such a program by means of a controlled experiment, those rules would be replaced by random assignment.

The government, however, may want to assure that at least high-priority cases continue to receive the service. Those cases generally would have to be excluded from the experiment so as not to confound the comparisons, which otherwise would reflect the greater presence of those clients in the treated group than in the control group.

To get around this problem, clients can be classified as to the extent to which they need assistance. Those clearly in need would be given the service, those clearly not in need would not be given the service, and both groups would be excluded from the experiment.[7]

6. *The risk in funding the program without a controlled experiment is likely to be substantially greater than the cost of the experiment; the new program involves large costs and a large degree of uncertainty.* A controlled experiment can be costly. It generally requires careful planning prior to implementation of the new program. It also requires special data collection procedures and careful attention during the period of the experiment to obtain the needed data and to make sure that the experimental procedures are maintained.

---

6. For a further discussion of this point, see Reference 7. For some services, such as social casework, the service's inherent effectiveness has been severely questioned; see Reference 16, which reviews the findings of a number of past evaluations of casework including some controlled experiments.

7. Reference 7.

The general principle is that the costs of the experiment—both political and fiscal—should be substantially less than the value of the savings or of the improved benefits likely to accrue because the experiment was undertaken. (Such a judgment, of course, can be difficult to make in advance.)

Good candidates for controlled experiments are new programs that are costly and that, once in place, are likely to be extremely difficult to terminate, cut back, or even modify. In such cases the use of a test period to evaluate the program on less than a full-scale basis (if possible) is likely to be particularly appropriate. A test period may reduce (but will not eliminate) the creation of the strong interest groups that are likely to form when a full-scale program is initiated. Decisions about continuation of the program after the test period can then be made in a more objective environment.

To the extent that there is considerable risk or substantial cost involved in moving ahead with full-scale implementation, experimentation should be considered as a way to temporize and to obtain needed information to reduce the overall risk and long-run expense. If a weaker evaluation design is used instead, there will be a greater likelihood that incorrect decisions will be made.

7. *A decision to implement the program can be postponed until the experiment is completed.* A full experiment can require a substantial amount of time, typically at least a year and possibly two or three or even more. An experiment should be considered if a decision on full-scale implementation can be postponed until the experimental findings are available. When decisions on implementation are needed quickly, an experiment is unlikely to be feasible.

Usually at least one or two years are needed for controlled experiments, but this is not always the case. The introduction of new equipment or new small-scale procedures whose impacts can be expected to appear quickly may offer opportunities for experiments that last less than a year.

If there is considerable political pressure to provide a new service (perhaps in response to a recent emergency), and it is difficult to delay full-scale implementation, experimentation will be difficult to apply. The experimental approach, however, can be a way to temporize when public officials feel that full-scale implementation would be primarily an emotional response that could turn out to be quite wasteful.

There are also other elements that can make it difficult to postpone full-scale program implementation while undertaking an experiment. An experiment may not be appropriate, for example, if the program requires a major capital investment, so that a significant savings could not be obtained by the temporizing experiment (e.g., local governments are not likely to find it appropriate to experiment with different kinds of water treatment plants). Similarly, governments are unlikely to experiment if implementation of a program would require a major upheaval in organization.

The generalization here is that the experimental approach will be considerably less attractive if a large investment (whether capital or human) is required that cannot be scaled down for an experiment and, once done, is very difficult to undo.

8. *Experimental conditions can be maintained reasonably well during the experimental period.* It can be quite difficult to maintain experimental conditions during the life of an experiment. It is probably impossible to maintain them exactly for any length of time. Program personnel are frequently tempted to deviate from the original concept and to introduce other elements into the program, thus contaminating the experiment. The experimental design becomes less feasible to the extent that:

- the experimental program requires program staff to adhere closely to unusual procedures;
- the random assignment of persons or units to the control and experimental groups can be affected if the evaluators are "not looking"'
- the experiment is to be continued over a very long period of time, increasing the probability of deviation from the plan.

Experiments are less likely to be contaminated, if random assignments are made only at the beginning of the experiment, or at only a few known points in time.

A major concern is the degree to which program personnel will be able to bypass the requirements of the experimental design. Experiments that depend heavily on unusual actions by program personnel or clients are particularly vulnerable. These problems can be prevented to some extent by proper preparation of the experiment and by close control of program activities, but this is often difficult. What is evident, however, is that experimental programs that can be handled relatively unobtrusively—in the sense that they cannot easily be aborted by program personnel (or by clients)—are better candidates for this evaluation design.

9. *The findings are likely to be generally applicable to a substantial proportion of the population of interest.* The purpose of an experiment is to indicate whether the program being evaluated (or

some version of it) is sufficiently meritorious to be continued, and whether it should be applied to the whole client population or to some major segment of it. This means that the control and experimental groups should be representative of the future client population, and the circumstances of the experiment should be as representative as possible of anticipated conditions. If there is considerable doubt that these two objectives can be achieved, an experiment may not be appropriate.

Some specific problems that can abort or reduce the value of an experiment are listed below. If these conditions cannot be avoided, or at least minimized, the data from the experiment will become difficult to interpret.

- The experiment does not include all major types of clients, or most of the major conditions under which the program will be expected to operate.
- Special personnel have to be used for the experiment, or the personnel are likely to be particularly motivated or particularly capable, and the performance of such personnel is important to the outcomes. The use of special, highly motivated, or especially capable persons in an experiment should generally be avoided. (Early team policing experiments made use of volunteer officers, but even though the new teams were randomly assigned to "matched" precincts the use of more highly motivated public officers was criticized as prejudicing the experiment in favor of the teams.)
- The experimental or control group or groups must be made aware of the experiment and are likely to behave in unusual ways, leading to outcomes that are not likely to be representative of general conditions.
- The program personnel know of the experiment and are likely to act in unusual ways that are not part of the planned procedures, so that the outcomes are not likely to be representative. This problem is particularly troublesome when it arises in programs where program personnel play a major role in the outcome.

The latter problems suggest that an experiment should be relatively unobtrusive and last long enough so that the novelty of the situation will wear off. If feasible and ethical, it is preferable that the persons involved in the experiment not be aware of it. This is often not possible, but at least the visibility and obtrusiveness of the experiment should be minimized. There is, in general, less probability that the control group will act in an unusual manner during the experiment, since their situation ordinarily remains the same as it was before the experiment. Even here, however, a high-visibility experiment may initiate unusual behavior by the control group or by employees dealing with it. Program personnel who learned that a new program was being tried at other locations, for example, might try to provide the same service to their own clients (the control group).

10. *Sufficient staff and dollars are available to manage the experiment.* A controlled experiment requires careful attention and monitoring. Administrators, and even experienced evaluators, often underestimate the cost and effort required for even a modest one. Substantial resources may be needed, both to be sure that the proper data are collected and that experimental conditions are maintained throughout the experiment. Data from a poorly managed or inadequately financed design can be worse than no data at all.

11. *Client consent for participation in the experiment is not required or, if it is, can be obtained without invalidating the experiment.* In some experiments it is necessary for clients to give their consent. If a significant proportion of the clients can be expected not to consent, or if the request for consent can be expected to alter clients' behavior in a way that reduces the general applicability of the findings, an experimental design is not appropriate.

Consent is not always necessary, particularly for programs that do not involve direct services to individual clients. In the Kansas City police patrol experiment, for example, it was not deemed necessary to obtain permission from residents of the areas where standard police patrols were withdrawn. In a Baltimore experiment that tested financial and job placement help as ways to reduce recidivism among ex-convicts, it was not felt necessary to tell them they were part of an experiment. They were not told anything about either the financial aid or job placement help that they would be receiving, but only to report to a particular office. The purpose was to keep the stimulus of the first visit the same for all of the ex-convicts, regardless of their subsequent assignment to the experimental or control group.[8]

A study of the use of random assignment in twelve experiments found that in half of them the randomization procedure was explained and, in general, accepted by the clients. The experiment that

---

8. See Reference 82.

encountered the greatest problem was a federally sponsored experiment that provided desegregation funds to treatment schools and no funds to control schools. The schools were aware of the situation, and many complaints resulted after the selections. As a compromise, some funds were then provided to a few of the control schools. This weakened the contrast between the control and the treatment schools but maintained the basic design.[9]

12. *The confidentiality and privacy of the clients involved can be adequately maintained.* Evaluation experiments involving treatment for individual clients generally include the obtaining of personal information on the clients. Unless the information can be obtained without unacceptable intrusions on client privacy and maintained in confidence, the experiment should not be undertaken. The anonymity of individual clients can be preserved by proper procedures, and the findings of the experiment should only be presented in the form of aggregative statistics. Identifying information on particular clients should be deleted after the evaluation has been completed.

The need to protect confidentiality applies to all evaluation designs but can be more troublesome in controlled experiments, in which substantial numbers of clients may be involved over extended periods of time.

---

9. See Reference 12, particularly p. 229 ff.

REFERENCES

Evaluation and Its Techniques

1. Anderson, Scarvia B., and Ball, Samuel. *The Profession and Practice of Program Evaluation.* San Francisco, California: Jossey-Bass, Inc., 1978.
2. Attkisson, C. Clifford; Hargreaves, William A.; Horowitz, William A.; Sorensen, James E.; eds., *Evaluation of Human Service Programs.* New York: Academic Press, 1978.
3. Babbie, Earl R. "Survey Research Methods." Belmont, California: Wadsworth Publishing Co., Inc., 1973.
4. Bernstein, Ilene N.; Borhnstedt, George W.; and Borgatta, Edgar F. "External Validity and Evaluation Research: A Codification of Problems." *Sociological Methods and Research.* Vol. 4, No. 1, August 1975.
5. Blair, Louis H., and Schwartz, Alfred I. *How Clean is our City?* Washington, D.C.: The Urban Institute, 1972.
6. Boots, Andrew III., et al. *Inequality in Local Government Services: A Case Study of Neighborhood Roads.* Washington, D.C.: The Urban Institute, 1972.
7. Boruch, Robert F. "On Common Contentions About Randomized Field Experiments." *Evaluation Studies Review Annual.* Vol. 1, 1976.
8. Campbell, Donald T. "Reforms as Experiments." *Urban Affairs Quarterly.* December 1976. (Reprinted from the *American Psychologist.* Vol. 24, No. 4, April 1969, pp. 409–429.)
9. Campbell, Donald T., and Ross, H. Laurence. "The Connecticut Crackdown on Speeding: Time-Series Data in Quasi-Experimental Analysis." *Law Society and Review.* Vol. 2, pp. 33–53, August 1968.
10. Campbell, Donald T., and Stanley, Julian C. *Experimental and Quasi-Experimental Designs for Research.* Chicago: Rand McNally and Company, 1966.
11. Clarren, Sumner N.; Woodward, Jane P.; and Hatry, Harry P. *Improving the Usefulness of Program Analysis and Evaluation Activities in Local Government: A Guidebook.* Washington,

118

D.C.: The Urban Institute, 1978. (Available from National Technical Information Service, HUD #0000469.)

12. Conner, Ross F. "Selecting A Control Group: An Analysis of the Randomization Process in Twelve Social Reform Programs." *Evaluation Quarterly.* Vol. 1, No. 2, May 1977.

13. Cook, Thomas D., and Campbell, Donald ˙T. *Quasi-Experimentation: Design & Analysis Issues for Field Settings.* Chicago: Rand McNally College Publishing Co., 1979.

14. Evaluation Research Society. "Standards for Program Evaluation." (Exposure Draft), May 1980.

15. Fanshel, David. "Computerized Information Systems and Foster Care: The New York City Experience with CWIS." *Children Today.* Nov/Dec 1976.

16. Fischer, Joel. *The Effectiveness of Social Casework.* Springfield, Illinois: Charles C Thomas, 1976.

17. Fisk, Donald M., et al. "How Effective Are Your Community Recreation Services." For the Bureau of Outdoor Recreation, U.S. Department of Interior, April 1973. (Available from the Government Printing Office, Washington, D.C., Stock No. 024-016-0055-0.)

18. Fitz-Gibbon, Carol Taylor, and Morris, Lynn Lyons. "How to Design a Program Evaluation." Beverly Hills, California: Sage Publications, 1978.

19. Geismar, Ludwig L. *Family and Community Functioning, A Manual of Measurement for Social Work Practice and Policy.* Metuchen, New Jersey: Scarecrow Press, Inc., 1971.

20. Greiner, John M., Hall, John R., et al. *Monitoring the Effectiveness of State Transportation Services.* Washington, D.C.: The Urban Institute, July 1977.

21. Hall, John R. "Factors Related to Local Government Use of Performance Measurement." April 1978. (Available from the Office of Policy Development and Research, U.S. Department of Housing and Urban Development, HUD-PDR-396, May 1979; also available from the National Technical Information Service, Order No. PB 300241.)

22. Harrington, Phillip J., and Sanders, James R. "Guidelines for Goal-Free Evaluation." Evaluation Center, Western Michigan University, June 1979.

23. Hatry, Harry P.; Clarren, Sumner N.; and van Houten, Therese, et al. *Efficiency Measurement for Local Government Services: Some Initial Suggestions.* Washington, D.C.: The Urban Institute, November 1979.

24. Hatry, Harry P., et al. *How Effective Are Your Community Services? Procedures for Monitoring the Effectiveness of Municipal Services.* Washington, D.C.: The Urban Institute and the International City Management Association, 1977.

25. Koss, Margo; Hatry, Harry P.; Millar, Annie., et al., *Social Services: What Happens to the Clients?* Washington, D.C.: The Urban Institute, December 1979.

26. Levitan, Sar A., and Wurzburg, Gregory. *Evaluating Federal Social Programs: An Uncertain Art.* Kalamazoo, Michigan: W. E. Upjohn Institute for Employment Research, 1979.

27. Levy, Clifford V. *A Primer for Community Research.* Far West Research Inc., San Francisco, California, 1972.

28. MacGregor, Gay, and St. George, Arthur. *Evaluation of State and Local Programs: A Primer.* Santa Fe, New Mexico, New Mexico State Planning Office, November 1, 1976.

29. Mitchell, Glen H. *Conducting the Consumer Survey — A Primer for Volunteers.* Virginia Polytechnic Institute and State University Extension Division. Blacksburg, Virginia, June 1979.

30. Morris, Lynn Lyons, and Fitz-Gibbon, Carol Taylor. *How to Measure Program Implementation.* Beverly Hills, California: Sage Publications, 1978.

31. Morris, Lynn Lyons, and Fitz-Gibbon, Carol Taylor. *How to Present an Evaluation Report.* Beverly Hills, California: Sage Publications, 1978.

32. Ostrom, Elinor, *Multi-Mode Approaches to the Measurement of Government Productivity.* Department of Political Science, Indiana University, Bloomington, 1975.

33. Patton, Michael Quinn. *Utilization Focused Evaluation.* Beverly Hills, California: Sage Publications, 1978.

34. Public Technology, Inc., *Program Evaluation and Analysis: A Management Report for State and Local Governments,* and *Program Evaluation and Analysis: A Technical Guide for State and Local Governments.* Office of Policy Development and Research, U.S. Department of Housing and Urban Development, 1978. (Available from U.S. Government Printing Office, Washington, D.C.)

35. Riecken, Henry W., and Boruch, Robert F. *Social Experimentation: A Method for Planning and Evaluating Social Intervention.* New York: Academic Press, Inc., 1974.

36. Rivlin, Alice M. *Systematic Thinking for Social Action.* Washington, D.C.: The Brookings Institution, 1971.

37. Roos, Noralou P. "Contrasting Social Experimentation with Retrospective Evaluation: A Health Care Perspective." *Public Policy.* Vol. 23, No. 2, Spring 1975.

38. Rossi, Peter H.; Freeman, Howard E.; and Wright, Sonia R. *Evaluation: A Systematic Approach.* Beverly Hills, California: Sage Publications, 1979.

39. Schainblatt, Alfred H., and Hatry, Harry P. *Mental Health Services: What Happens to the Clients?* Washington, D.C.: The Urban Institute, December 1979.

40. Schmidt, Richard E.; Scanlon, John W.; and Bell, James B. *Evaluability Assessment: Making Public Programs Work Better.* Washington, D.C.: Project SHARE, Human Services Monograph Series No. 14, November 1979.

41. Scriven, Michael. "Goal Free Evaluation Practice." Presented at the Council Meeting of the American Educational Research Association, Toronto, Canada, 1978.

42. State-Local Finance Project. "Planning-Programming-Budgeting System Note 6: The Role and Nature of Cost Analysis in the PPB System." George Washington University, Washington, D.C., 1968.

43. Suchman, Edward A. *Evaluation Research: Principles and Practice in Public Service & Social Action Programs.* New York: Russell Sage Foundation, 1967.

44. The Urban Institute and The International City Management Association. "The Challenge of Productivity Diversity: Improving Local Government Productivity Measurement and Evaluation," June 1972. (Available from the National Technical Information Service, Order No. PB 223114.)

45. U.S. Civil Service Commission. "Construction of Questionnaires." Technical Study No. TS-7-73-1, Washington, D.C., July 1973.

46. U.S. General Accounting Office. "Standards for Audit of Governmental Organizations, Programs, Activities, and Functions." Washington, D.C., 1972.

47. Webb, Kenneth, and Hatry, Harry P. *Obtaining Citizen Feedback: The Application of Citizen Surveys to Local Governments.* Washington, D.C.: The Urban Institute, 1973.

48. Weiss, Carol H. *Evaluating Action Programs: Reading in Social Action and Education.* Boston: Allyn and Bacon, Inc., 1972.

49. Weiss, Carol H. *Evaluation Research: Methods of Assessing Program Effectiveness.* Englewood Cliffs, New Jersey: Prentice-Hall, Inc., 1972.

50. Weiss, Carol H., and Hatry, Harry P. *An Introduction to Sample Surveys for Government Managers.* Washington, D.C.: The Urban Institute, March 1971.
51. Wholey, Joseph S. *Evaluation: Promise and Performance.* Washington, D.C.: The Urban Institute, 1979.
52. Wholey, Joseph S., et al. *Federal Evaluation Policy: Analyzing the Effects of Public Programs.* Washington, D.C.: The Urban Institute, 1970.
53. Winnie, Richard E., and Hatry, Harry P. *Measuring the Effectiveness of Local Government Services: Transportation.* Washington, D.C.: The Urban Institute, 1972.
54. Wise, Lois Recascino. "Evaluating the Impact of Public Programs: A Guide to Evaluative Research." Midwest Intergovernmental Training Committee, Bloomington, Indiana, 1978.

**Examples and Case Studies of State and
Local Government Evaluations**
55. Alameda, County of. "Evaluation of Alcoholism Treatment Alternatives: A Client Follow-up: Final Report." Office of Program Evaluation, Oakland, California, July 1977.
56. Burt, Marvin R.; and Blair, Louis H. *Options for Improving the Care of Neglected and Dependent Children.* Washington, D.C.: The Urban Institute, March 1971.
57. Burt, Marvin R.; Blair, Louis H.; Scott, H.; and McKelvey, C.P. "Dade County Drug Abuse Treatment System Policy Analysis." Office of the County Manager, Metropolitan Dade County, Florida, 1972.
58. Charlotte, City of. "CETA Contract Evaluation Report for the In-School Career-Employment Program." Budget and Evaluation Department, Charlotte, North Carolina, 1979.
59. Charlotte, City of. Community Development Program Evaluation Report of the "Hot Meals for the Elderly Program," Budget and Evaluation Department, Charlotte, North Carolina, January 14, 1977.
60. Ciaburn, W. Eugene, and Magura, Stephen. "Administrative Case Review for Foster Children." *Social Work Research and Abstracts,* Vol. 14, No. 1, Spring 1978.
61. District of Columbia. "How Does Pretrial Supervision Affect Pretrial Performance?" D.C. Bail Agency, Washington, D.C., May 1978.
62. Fisk, Donald M. "The Indianapolis Police Fleet Plan." The Urban Institute, Washington, D.C., October 1970.

122

63. Florida, State of. "Youth Services Probation and Diversion Study." Department of Health and Rehabilitation Services. Tallahassee, Florida, June 20, 1977.
64. Kelling, George, et al. "The Kansas City Preventive Patrol Experiment." Police Foundation, Washington, D.C., October 1974.
65. Michigan, State of. "Bay County Employment and Training Study." Office of Planning, Budget and Evaluation, Michigan Department of Social Services, November 9, 1979.
66. New York, City of. "The State Training and Manpower Program Performance Audit." Office of the Comptroller, New York, New York, November 25, 1977.
67. New York City Citizens Budget Commission. "A Review of New York City's Management Program: CBC Update Number 2." New York City, October 1979.
68. New York State. Legislative Commission on Expenditure Review. "Parole Resource Centers Program." Albany, New York, August 1979.
69. New York State. Legislative Commission on Expenditure Review. "Persons Released from State Developmental Centers." Albany, New York, December 18, 1975.
70. Pennsylvania, State of. "Program Audit Report on Vocational Training in Pennsylvania State Correctional Institutions." Division of Program Audit, Office of the Budget, October 1970.
71. Pennsylvania, State of. "An Evaluation of the Production and Cost of Highway Maintenance in Pennsylvania." Division of Program Planning and Evaluation, Office of the Budget, Harrisburg, Pennsylvania, July 1978.
72. Pennsylvania, State of. "An Evaluation of the Traffic Supervision Program." Division of Planning and Program Evaluation. Office of the Budget, Harrisburg, Pennsylvania, March 1976.
73. Phoenix, City of. "Mechanized Contained Refuse Collection System (RAPID-RAIL)." Budget and Research Department Research Report No. 75–4, Phoenix, Arizona, July 26, 1974.
74. Phoenix, City of. "Overall ASAP Progress: Annual Report Section One." Management and Budget Department, Phoenix, Arizona, June 1978.
75. Phoenix, City of. "Evaluation of Police 'Emergency Only' Cars." Office of Management and Budget, City Council Report No. MB 77–107, Phoenix, Arizona, 1977.
76. Portland, City of. "Dental Health Program Evaluation." Third Year Report, Portland, Maine, December 1979.

77. San Diego, County of. "Evaluation of the San Diego County Aid for Families With Dependent Children Program." Office of Program Evaluation, San Diego, California, May 23, 1977.

78. San Diego, County of. "Evaluation of the San Diego County Food Stamp Program." Office of Program Evaluation, San Diego, California, March 3, 1975.

79. Virginia, State of. "Program Evaluation: Virginia Drug Abuse Control Programs." Joint Legislative Audit and Review Commission, October 14, 1975.

80. Virginia, State of. "Program Evaluation: Vocational Rehabilitation in Virginia." Joint Legislative Audit and Review Commission, November 9, 1976.

81. Wilmington, City of. "A Study of Alternative Approaches to Motor Vehicle Maintenance." Department of Planning and Development, Wilmington, Delaware, 1977.

82. Lenihan, Kenneth J., and Casey, Florence M. "Unlocking the Second Gate: The Role of Financial Assistance in Reducing Recidivism Among Ex-Prisoners." Employment and Training Administration, U.S. Department of Labor, Washington, D.C., 1977.

83. U.S. National Center for Productivity and Quality of Working Life. "Improving Government Productivity: Selected Case Studies." Spring 1977, U.S. Government Printing Office, Stock No. 052-003-00353-8.